SURFACE ARCHITECTURE

SURFACE ARCHITECTURE

DAVID LEATHERBARROW AND MOHSEN MOSTAFAVI

THE MIT PRESS   CAMBRIDGE, MASSACHUSETTS   LONDON, ENGLAND

This book was set in Bembo and Engravers Gothic BT by Achorn Graphic Services Inc., and was printed and bound in the United States of America.

Library of Congress Cataloging-in-Publication Data

Leatherbarrow, David.
   Surface architecture / David Leatherbarrow and Mohsen Mostafavi.
      p. cm.
   Includes bibliographical references and index.
   ISBN 0-262-13407-1 (hc. : alk. paper)
   1. Architecture. 2. Architecture and technology. 3. Materials—Appearance. I. Mostafavi, Mohsen. II. Title.

NA2540 .L36 2002
720′.1′05—dc21

                                                    2001056834

CONTENTS

ACKNOWLEDGMENTS

This book was written in and between Cambridge (Massachusetts), London, and Philadelphia. Universities and schools in each of these cities supported our work; especially helpful were staff members at libraries and archives of the Architectural Association, Harvard University, and the University of Pennsylvania. The illustrations in this volume were assembled by Sarah Franklin and Sarah Farmer under the guidance of Valerie Bennett. Funds that contributed to the preparation of these illustrations were provided by Penn's Department of Architecture, thanks to Richard Wesley. We would also like to thank Pamela Johnston, Mark Rappolt, and Mary Wall for their editorial advice. In addition to this, we were greatly assisted by a number of students who served as research assistants: Paul Emmons, Gordana Kostich, Carlos Naranjo, Tonkao Panin, and Franca Trubiano. The book's themes benefited greatly as a result of discussions with Homa Fardjadi, Brett Steele, Irénée Scalbert, and Richard Wesley, while early drafts were improved following the comments and criticism of a number of scholars whose publications were important to us. We are particularly grateful to Edward Ford. At the MIT Press, Roger Conover provided unwavering guidance and support; many thanks also to Matthew Abbate and Yasuyo Iguchi for their editorial and design work, respectively. Above all, this book would not have been possible without the generosity and the forgiveness of Homa Fardjadi and Lauren Leatherbarrow.

SURFACE ARCHITECTURE

INTRODUCTION: WHY SURFACE ARCHITECTURE?

Production and representation are in conflict in contemporary architectural practice. For the architect, the mass production of building elements has led to an ever-increasing source of materials from which to configure an architectural project. The built outcome of such a configuration largely results, however, in representations that oscillate between visual reflections of systems of production and pictorial recollections of earlier styles and motifs. The first practice mimics machine assembly—reproduction—and the second pictures an architecture based on earlier and outdated modes of construction. These practices are problematic in two senses: buildings that relinquish their appearance to the image that results from assembly processes neglect the *project* of representation, and the picturing of historical profiles in nostalgic recollection ignores the opportunities for new configurations based on the availability of both new and old materials and methods of building construction.

To speak of the project of representation is to recognize the problematics of appearance. In one sense this is not a new phenomenon specific to contemporary architecture. After all, the discussion on the question of style, epitomized by such texts as Heinrich Hübsch's *In What Style Shall We Build?,* had already begun in the nineteenth century. Yet the arguments concerning contemporary architecture, its construction in general, and its appearance in particular have not given this topic the same degree of attention. Furthermore, there is a greater ambiguity regarding the parameters for such a discussion today. Architecture's becoming, the correlation between its processes of construction and its appearance, has to be reconsidered. In this context, representation cannot be limited to the communicability of the image.

A good example of this conflict between construction and appearance is the work of the American architect Albert Kahn. His is an architecture that vividly demonstrates the symmetrical but divided commitment to production and representation that has come to be typical of our time.

Kahn is best known and frequently praised as a designer of factory buildings during the early part of the twentieth century. But this type of construction was not the only one that occupied his attention, nor one that he saw as essentially architectural, despite the way apologists for high modernism have interpreted his buildings. Throughout his long and exceedingly productive career, Kahn never doubted the distinction between what he called the art of architecture and the business of building. Projects he would have included in the former category were his designs for churches and synagogues, schools, libraries, residences, and so on. Examples of this kind of work fill about half of his 1948 publication of his own works. Projects he included in the latter category, the business of building, are factories of all sorts, production buildings, boiler houses, and other examples of industrial architecture—ironically, the only types of buildings included in George Nelson's 1939 publication on Kahn's work. If we compare the designs in each category, the distinction between architectural "art" and "business" could not be stronger, nor more obvious; the latter accommodates and conforms to the logic of industrial production, the former to the aspirations and conventional motifs of representation. The clear separation of these tasks was not new to Kahn, however; it was already common in the nineteenth century, in the context of industrialization when new typologies, such as the railway station, had to mediate between the products of industrialization and the public realm—between engineering and architecture.

Even though it has become common to interpret the alternative between industrial production and representation in stylistic terms, such an understanding can be misleading, since it assumes that architectural solutions to economic requirements have their own style, the modern style. Albert Kahn never saw his factory buildings as possessed of a style, one that would be for modern times what the Renaissance and baroque manners had been for earlier epochs. The exception to this, perhaps, would be the front part of his factories, the part that housed the entry lobby and offices for the managers, which were given treatments that exceeded the requirements of functional concerns—they were "streamlined."

In his forceful criticism of modern architecture, Albert Kahn rejected the premise that the new architecture of steel and glass would be adequate to the

1.1

Albert Kahn, Ford Motor Company,
glass plant, Detroit, 1922.

1.2
Albert Kahn, Ford Motor Company,
air station, Detroit, 1922.

1.3

Albert Kahn, Ford Motor Company,
engineering laboratory, Detroit, 1922.

several tasks of accommodating and representing the full range of architectural concerns, those that were fundamental to inherited culture. The inadequacy of the new materials and methods could be seen when a building by a modern architect was compared with one by someone practicing within the classical tradition. His rejection of buildings by Le Corbusier, Lurçat, and Mallet-Stevens in France, or those by Mendelsohn, Poelzig, and Gropius in Germany, was complemented by his praise of the works of architects trained in the Beaux-Arts manner, such as Charles McKim, after whose designs Kahn's own Clements Library (his favorite building) may well have been modeled.

Yet while *style* may not be the best category to use when making a distinction between Kahn's industrial and nonindustrial buildings, *history* may be. In his rejection of modern solutions for institutional projects, Kahn denounced the "radical abandonment of all that has served hitherto," meaning the accumulated wisdom and motifs of the great architecture of the past. Likewise, in praising McKim, he celebrated his "re-use of well-tried forms."[1] This was not meant to discredit industrial solutions, nor the modern methods and materials used in their construction; it was meant simply to distinguish modern modes and elements of production from the tasks and motifs that could properly be called architectural. Some types answer current and pressing needs, others acknowledge conditions that have been and will be significant in perpetuity. Because examples of the first kind are of the moment, and moments change, they must be flexible, adaptable, and extendable, as were Kahn's factories. The second kind results from the combination and composition of elements that have been used for long periods of time, and therefore should look familiar and appropriate, as did his institutional buildings. The distinction between industrial and nonindustrial building is essentially one that finds in contemporary technology solutions to contemporary problems, while finding in historical forms motifs that can be used for suitable solutions: the first is a matter of building production, "business," the second of architectural representation, "art."

The question, therefore, concerns the alternatives to this division between production and representation, which in some ways is also an extension of that between modernity and tradition. How can design utilize the opportunities of current industrial production so that the practice of architectural representation is neither independent of nor subjugated to the domination of technology?

This question, while of general concern to architecture, is most apparent and unavoidable in the design of the external surface of buildings. Traditionally,

technology

this was the problem of designing a facade. Yet, since the early part of the twentieth century, with the advent of the "free facade" and new technologies of construction, the nature and definition of the building's appearance became the subject of repeated consideration. As a result, the task of designing a "facade" has itself become questionable. Is this a loss? Or are there other ways of thinking and working with the topic that avoid dichotomy or the subjugation of one concern to the other? It may be that the unease with the facade also results from a suspicion about the project of representation itself. The task of disclosure in architecture is not limited to that of representation in the traditional sense of the word. An alternative strategy could involve seeing the building's external cladding as elements that structure both the building's skin and its temporal operations—an approach that would initially be seen as against representation.

One way of developing this question would be to pursue the reciprocity between the intentions behind an architectural project and the imperatives of construction, and in particular the role of technique. In contemporary architecture, process and methods of construction play an increasingly important role in the development and realization of many projects. It seems, therefore, that the historical position of mass production as one of the dominant factors of architectural "progress" requires rethinking. The fact that optimization through mass production did not result in the architectural benefits promised by its advocates suggests that the relationship between architecture and technology merits thought.

One of the strongest manifestations of an architecture of progress in the interwar and postwar period was the International Style. Already in its heyday this style received harsh criticism for its neglect of what was specific to locations or regions, a criticism that has led in recent years to proposals for a regionalist architecture. Some critics have demonstrated the inherently conservative character of the regionalist approach. Alan Colquhoun has shown a basic premise that all societies contain a "core, or essence, that must be discovered and preserved. One aspect of this essence lies in local geography, climate, and customs, involving the use and transformation of local, 'natural' materials."[2] He argues that this position can lead to the reinforcement of things as they are or have been rather than as they may become. This form of repetition accents history in the same way that style concerns promote well-tried or familiar motifs. Advocates of regionalism have, however, proposed it as a strategy and politics of resistance.[3] Clearly, engagement with particularities is one way the domination of technology can be interrupted. The motives for these strategies may include the desire to affirm cultural conditions that are both inherited and contemporary; yet the conflict persists.

Built works and projects can be used to clarify these questions, as can writings, particularly those from the late nineteenth century to the present. The concern with the difficulties and opportunities of the external surface of buildings begins with the theoretical and practical isolation of that surface as the subject matter of architectural design. The autonomy of the surface, the "free facade," presumes a distinction between the structural and nonstructural elements of the building, between the frame and the cladding. This distinction is vividly present in the architecture of turn-of-the-century Chicago.

The discovery of the free facade was accompanied by unprecedented transformations in its tectonic and material qualities. Before the widespread use of frame construction, requirements for light, ventilation, and views outside the building were met with apertures, built as openings in a wall. The limits of these openings affirmed the wall's tectonic and theoretical primacy. The frame changed all of that: windows ceased being openings in walls and became walls themselves. But when this occurred, the wall's non-load-bearing functions had to be reconsidered. This redefinition of the tasks of enclosure at times achieved opposite ends. The use of transparent glass, for example, accomplished tasks previously associated with opacity. Not only considerations of light, ventilation, and view come into this, but also problems of appearance and construction. In fact, the use of standardized elements of construction highlights not only the difficulty of placing windows in walls but the more general issue of architectural surfaces.

Once the skin of the building became independent of its structure, it could just as well hang like a curtain or clothing. The relationship between structure and skin has preoccupied much architectural production since this period and remains contested today. The site of this contest is the architectural surface.

the problem of skin itself should be reconsidered as well,

FRAMING THE FACE

A commonplace of architectural history and criticism holds that the embrace of industrialization and its products in twentieth-century architecture led to the abandonment of the project of representation in architecture and of the primary instrument of representation—the facade. Were this indeed the case, it would mean the end of a very long-standing tradition, for the idea of the facade as a distinct representational face of the building has existed since the late medieval and early Renaissance periods.

The fact that there was often a temporal separation between the construction of the main building enclosure and the facade of many Renaissance churches points to the partial autonomy of the facade as bearer of signifactory attributes.[1] This delay led to a categorical distinction between a building's walls and its facade, or face, the latter being its most expressive part. And what began during the early Renaissance has continued up until our time.

In the eighteenth century, a number of architects theorized the expressive value of architectural *physiognomies*. Key figures in this development were Germain Boffrand, Jacques-François Blondel, Nicolas Le Camus de Mézières, Etienne-Louis Boullée, and Claude-Nicolas Ledoux. Boffrand and Blondel, for example, utilized concepts elaborated in the theory of pictorial physiognomy; specifically, the idea that there exists a direct correspondence between the profile of a face and the theme or genre of a representation, whether a picture or a building.[2] "All emotions [for Boffrand] could be expressed in architecture."[3] Three basic line forms, the convex, concave, and the straight, were understood as the means of expression. Boffrand made no mention of Charles Le Brun, but there can be little doubt that he had his ideas in mind when he castigated the architects of the early eighteenth century for designing interiors with lines "intertwined to confusion" and for not understanding that lines are to architecture what tones are to music. By means of the three line forms, and with knowledge of typical expressions, the skilled architect might strike chords of sadness or joy, love or hate, grace or terror.[4]

By the time of Boullée and Ledoux, however, character had become more than the expression of genre by means of an indicative trace; the building's whole volume took on the role of character formation. Referred to as *architecture parlante,* this "speaking" architecture was thought to have reformative qualities capable of reshaping society.[5] The outer surfaces of the building now conveyed its functions more literally, making the totality of its surfaces and profiles a comprehensive site of representation. Architecture was made into an instrument of social morality, an agency of character building, no matter whether the object of "fabrication" was an individual or a group. The title of Ledoux's treatise makes this new role apparent: *Architecture Considered in Relation to Art, Morals, and Legislation.* Taxonomies of character, when transparent, were to allow not only for social inclusion but also for the exclusion of certain types. Ledoux's contemporary, the physiognomist Lavater, also focused on the literal correlations between facial profiles and a person's deviant behavior, intending, it seems, the identification of characters to be avoided. This speculation occurred in England as well as in France: the facade of Newgate Prison in London, designed by George Dance the Younger, utilized tectonic means to achieve a representation that indicated the building's purpose or "destination"; the facade inscription "spoke" of the horrors of incarceration and served the "function" of deterrence.[6] In this example, profile was thought not only to represent or express but to have an effect on the spectator. The theory of sensation, previously a matter of epistemology, became instrumental, suggesting how architectural images could accomplish social reform. Despite this premise, there is no evidence that these facades "worked" in the manner intended.

Nevertheless, so intense was the concentration on the signifying and "therapeutic" potential of the building's physiognomy that by the end of the nineteenth century it became possible, indeed normal, to think of this architectural element as "free"; not the "free facade" of Le Corbusier—free from the requirements and formal consequences of load-bearing structure—but independent as a

2.1
George Dance the Younger,
Newgate Prison, London, 1782.

site of representation, one that subordinated tectonic, topographical, and spatial to semiotic conditions. The architectural surface assumed a moral purpose. Early twentieth-century architects would accept and elaborate this premise. Le Corbusier himself, for example, argued that the whitewash of his early buildings allowed the outline of things to stand out from their background without any possibility of mistaken signification. He saw the contrast between the foreground objects and the background buildings as an X-ray of beauty. It is, he said, like a "court of assize in permanent session."[7]

The notion of objects standing in contrast to the building as background in part recalls Boullée's discussions of the "architecture of shadows," except that in his case the entire building participated in the play of atmospheric darks and lights. In *Architecture: Essay on Art,* Boullée recounted the time when he stood on the edge of a wood in the moonlight and caught a glimpse of his own shadow: "Because of my particular mood, the image seemed to me of an extreme melancholy. The shadows of the trees etched on the ground made a most profound impression on me. My imagination exaggerated the scene, and thus I had a glimpse of all that is somber in nature. What did I see there? The mass of the objects stood in black against the extreme wanness of the light. Nature offered itself to my gaze in mourning. I was struck by the sensations I was experiencing and immediately began to wonder how to apply this, especially to architecture."[8] Boullée's account of this "architecture of shadows" occurs in a section on "Funerary Monuments or Cenotaphs," a type of building which for him, more than any other, asks for the "poetry of architecture." To achieve the appropriate melancholy condition, the building had to consist of a flat surface and be absolutely stripped of detail, "its decoration consisting of a play of shadows, outlined by still deeper shadows."[9]

While a number of historians have described the similarities between this architecture and that of the early twentieth century, there is a clear and important difference: despite the flatness and unornamented character of these Enlightenment facades, never did their architects relinquish the task of having their compositions "speak" or perform social roles. It was precisely this expressive or rhetorical function and responsibility that the facades of the early twentieth century put into question. The emphasis on volume, which was identified by Philip Johnson and Henry-Russell Hitchcock as a defining characteristic of International Style architecture, is a well-known and significant indication of the decreased emphasis on the facade: "Thus the building is like a boat or umbrella

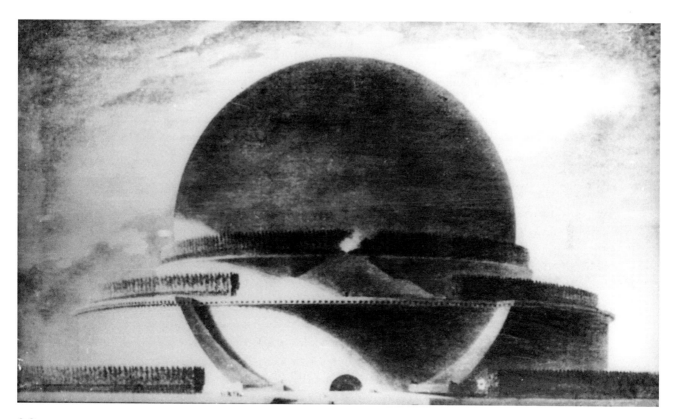

2.2

Etienne-Louis Boullée,
Cenotaph for Newton, 1784.

with strong internal support and a continuous outside covering. . . . Indeed, the great majority of buildings are in reality, as well as in effect, mere planes surrounding a volume . . . the glass of the windows is now an integral part of the enclosing screen rather than a hole in the wall."[10] While these authors proposed the use of glass cladding for expression of volume and flatness, the images they selected to illustrate this expression used ribbon or band windows and eliminated framing elements, such as cornices and bases. Among the very best examples were the department stores designed by Erich Mendelsohn. A more emphatic indication of the rejection of the distinct (and representational) facade was given by Theo van Doesburg, who attacked frontality and argued for an "all-sided development." From that time onward, the terms "face" and "elevation" have become interchangeable, and thus also began the tension between the building's "face" and its "frame."

MONUMENTAL VOLUMES

Despite the widespread acceptance of new and standardized methods of production in twentieth-century architecture, the idea of the facade as an instrument of representation has continued to be important, specifically in postwar American and European architectural debates. Representative instances of this are the conferences and publications of the Congrès Internationaux d'Architecture Moderne (CIAM), where the problems of reconstructing urban centers gave rise to questions about the appropriateness of modern architecture to the design of civic buildings, a traditional element of which was the facade. Sigfried Giedion's 1944 paper on monumentality, published in Paul Zucker's proceedings of a symposium on "New Architecture and City Planning," addressed the difficulties inherent in modern architecture's serving the representational purposes of civic design. Together with José Luis Sert and Fernand Léger, Giedion had introduced this question and related themes one year before under the title "Nine Points on Monumentality." In developing this argument, these three authors were not alone; many architects and critics had observed that while the early period of modern architecture had focused on housing, prefabrication, planning, and other architectural topics, it had not paid sufficient attention to questions of civic representation. Paul Zucker observed that modern architecture had passed through two phases: the first, at the turn of the century, was a time of "emancipation from the circle of eclectic imitation"; the second unveiled the prospect of "functional

2.3
Erich Mendelsohn,
Schocken Department Store,
Chemnitz, 1929.

expression." In the next phase to follow, architecture would be integrated with its "social aspect."[11] Zucker's historiography parallels Giedion's, for the latter also observed that modern architecture in its first phase had to start with the "single cell," that of the low-cost dwelling, and in its second phase had concentrated on urbanism. "The third phase lies ahead," Giedion wrote, warning that in "view of what had happened in the last century, and because of the way modern architecture had come into being, [this third phase will be] the most dangerous and the most difficult . . . the reconquest of the monumental expression."[12] Would this require the design of facades?

While the answer to this question is not simple, one issue was clear: the achievement of an architecture that went beyond functional expression would not involve regression to "pseudo monumentality." This, according to Giedion, had originated in the paper architecture of J. N. L. Durand, less in his buildings than in the designs set out in his *Précis des leçons d'architecture* (1801–1805). On the contrary, the "new monumentality" would challenge nineteenth- and twentieth-century examples of "pseudo monumentality." The latter was invariably achieved by placing a row of columns "in front of any building whatever its purpose and to whatever consequences it may lead."[13] For Giedion this indiscriminate practice was as evident in the Haus der Deutschen Kunst, commissioned by Adolf Hitler and completed in Munich in 1937, as it was in the Mellon Institute, built in the same year in Pittsburgh. But for Giedion there was no building more engulfed in the "pseudo ideals" of the nineteenth century than the Palace of the League of Nations in Geneva, finished in 1935: "perhaps the most distinguished example of internationally brewed eclecticism."[14] Eclecticism such as this illustrates the separation of figuration from construction. It was in this context that Joseph Hudnut, in 1949, introduced the term "post-modern."[15]

What, then, is the relationship between history and construction within the project of architectural representation? More specifically, can reference to history, to past forms and their respective traditions, take account of building "principles" (as Viollet-le-Duc had argued) or must it lead to direct imitation?

Postwar reconstruction itself raised questions concerning the production of monumental images. The reconstruction of Warsaw, for example, led by Helena and Szymon Syrkus, who were members of CIAM, was a very controversial project. At issue was the image of what was to be rebuilt: Should reconstruction aim at images of historical cities, or could civic monumentality be achieved through

2.4

Ludwig Troost, Haus der Deutschen
Kunst, Munich, 1937.

modern imagery? Is there a monumentality within modernity? Can modern architecture have a civic identity?

At the seventh meeting of CIAM in Bergamo in 1949, Helena Syrkus argued: "We do not need to fall into the eclecticism of drawing our material directly from the forms of the past but we should have a greater respect for the spirit of the past."[16] Because "mother Russia" encouraged the culture of each region, the "New Warsaw," the object of her continued dedication, would reflect neither the "Hitlerian 'Herrenvolk' mentality" nor the formalism of the "academic professors who employ eclectic forms." But would it be modern? Would it still be an architecture of volume, or does the reconsideration of "ancient culture" signal and presuppose a return to the (free) facade as the site of architectural representation? A few years before, in 1944, José Luis Sert, in his supplementary record of CIAM doctrine, introduced the related subjects of history and monumentality in his consideration of civic centers. Dismissing the "monuments of academic conception," he proposed that these centers would "summarize the aspirations of their populations." This would be in keeping with the historical function of such settings; yet their modernity would be achieved by an "amplitude of space," which implied, but did not state, an emphasis on volume, to the neglect of the "free facade."[17] When he returned to the subject in 1952, in one of his contributions to the publication of the eighth CIAM conference, *The Heart of the City,* he reiterated the (gentle) criticism of the early period of modern architecture, and the new emphasis on the social dimension of architecture and planning; but he added to these themes an argument for the nonfunctional aspects of "core" architecture, observing that "the need for the superfluous is as old as mankind."[18] Like Giedion, Sert did not recommend a return to applied historical motifs; instead, the development of elements that would add "a greater architectural expression, a richer plasticity, a more sculptural quality"—which is to say, a play of volumes, a task for architects to which the contributions of painters and sculptors might profitably be added. That this new plasticity could be achieved with modern methods and materials was meant to be obvious and was assumed in Sert's argument. It had also been the central theme of another paper on monumentality published in Zucker's collection: the paper put forward by Louis I. Kahn.

If monumentality is a spiritual quality that conveys a sense of eternity, as Kahn argued in the first lines of his paper, then architecture can (and will) achieve this through the building's structure and materials. Yet, while monumentality and the spirit are timeless, structure and materials, by contrast, are epochal; materials that are appropriate to our age are without precedent in ages past: "stimulated by [the scientific and technical] knowledge [of our time] we shall go far to develop the forms indigenous to our new materials and methods." To do so requires the risk of thinking monumentality anew: "no architect can *rebuild* a cathedral of another epoch . . . faithful duplication is unreconcilable [with current conditions]." Instead, architects must embrace the methods and materials of modern times. Kahn believed that modernity was vividly figured in contemporary industry, especially war industry: "war engineering achievements in concrete, steel and wood are showing the signs of maturity appropriate to guide the minds entrusted with the conception of [the cathedral of our time]. The giant major skeleton of the structure can assert its right to be seen. New wall products of transparent, translucent and opaque materials, with exciting textures and colors, [will be] suspended or otherwise fastened to the more delicate forms of the minor members."[19] All of these elements and more from modern science and technology were thought to give the architect the basis for new forms of collective life, the basis for a new cathedral, a new embodiment and image of the age.

If all of this seems clear and perhaps even unremarkable, by virtue of its similarity with other midcentury pronouncements, there is yet a difference in Kahn's account of modernity and construction. This difference was made especially clear a decade later in his famous "Order Is" prose poem, where his emphasis was not on modern means and materials alone—as if they were the (tectonic) expression of epochal consciousness—but on what might be called ahistorical or atemporal themes. These themes testify to the life of the spirit, to what is essential in the many and varied manifestations of building, which is to say "form."[20] He distinguished order, the "what," from design, the "how." The first emerges out of a system of construction but transcends it: "order is intangible. It is a level of creative consciousness forever becoming higher in level." Thus, while architectural order may express contemporary patterns or practices of collective or social agreement through design, more important and lasting is the embodiment of "ideas" internal to architecture and constitutive of all human associations—suggesting that monuments, or that sense of the spirit conveyed through monumental expression, do not persist in and through time but outside of time, that they manifest the desires not of a single age but of ages.

Does the preoccupation with "form" release architecture from the burden of acknowledging its history? Considering the line of argument or inference in

"Order Is," one might think so; yet, despite Kahn's essentializing in this and related texts, his writings and speeches are also filled with repeated references to antecedent examples—references to figures as historically distant as "Greek sculptors," Giotto, and Le Corbusier—as if his effort to transcend history depended on his success at appropriating it. Furthermore, his preoccupation with "form" was always tied to awareness of the constraints and opportunities of contemporary building; always assumed that the monuments and facades that were to escape history were necessarily bound to it, and that the relationship between construction and representation, like that between modernity and history, was inescapably conflictual. Thus a task: to discover expression and "form" within building production.

REPRESENTATION AND PRODUCTION

Let us, then, restate the problematic aspects of the current condition and suggest a way of considering it. The basic problem we want to address is the contested relationship between expression and technology. Our working premise is that the commonplace task of covering, dressing, or cladding an architectural construction is a particularly clear example of the conflict between representation and production in our time.

Elements of a contemporary cladding system can be seen either as fragments of a contemporary mode of production or as the constituents of facade iconography. The cladding panel focuses this conflict because it both conceals and reveals: as an industrial artifact it hides its own origin, as designed artifice it represents a larger body—the building itself. The question is: How can it be both? What is the relationship between an object originating in mass production and one intending aesthetic content? Is the cladding of a facade an outgrowth of its making, or is it something applied to the results of *mere* building? The subtle reciprocities and tensions between architectural figuration and rationalized industrial production have a decisive effect on architectural design and understanding; so much so that the nature and dilemma of contemporary architecture is revealed every time a building is covered in cladding.[21]

Within the logic of industrial production, cladding panels are entirely generic, capable of being "hung" on any number of buildings in any number of locations, elements of a truly "free" facade. Before construction, cladding panels reside in storage warehouses, standing "in reserve" for application. When they

2.5
Louis I. Kahn Alfred Newton Richards
Medical Building and Biology Building,
University of Pennsylvania,
Philadelphia, 1957–1964.
Photo: Julius Shulman.

enter into the construction of a building, however, these elements of a system lose their generality and become parts of an artifact that is wholly singular; when built, every construction exists in a particular location, for an individual client, and as a representation of a unique dwelling situation. How can cladding thus transform itself, how can it be both general and particular, suitable for the economies of construction, *repetition,* and the claims of representation, *identity?* When buildings utilizing mass-produced elements—modern office buildings, for example—were placed in the center of traditional towns, they obviously had "identity" or "singularity" because of their contrast with existing conditions, establishing identity through difference. But when these town centers were transformed through comprehensive "urban redevelopment," this sort of uniqueness was no longer apparent; instead, there was virtual sameness. The buildings that had been different soon became indistinguishable within an agglomeration; they became anonymous. But should the repetitive nature of mass production always result in a nameless or anonymous architecture? Anonymity is a complex issue. In the premodern or preindustrial city there are countless instances of buildings that exhibit repetitive elements. The row house, pervasive in many European and older American cities, is a good example. One can say further that as a construction type, the row house was virtually ubiquitous, and therefore anonymous. Does this anonymity differ from the twentieth-century case? How can we judge recent instances of repetitive construction sterile and alienating when we judge historical examples to be familiar and recognizable? Both result from typification, and this from abstraction. When is anonymity alienating and estranging, and when, to the contrary, is it reciprocating and community-defining?[22] It is impossible to assign negative value to all instances of typification, for everydayness also depends on typical actions and expressions. For architects active in the Bauhaus such as Hannes Meyer and Ludwig Hilberseimer, repetitive elements held the promise of a better society; yet for architects who have had to confront the cities built out of these elements, they have come to signify something quite different.

Generality in cladding results from the rationality of production, a principal tenet and technique of which is simplification. As implied in mass production, simplification does not sustain complexity but is dominated by the reductive processes necessary for mechanized reproduction. This form of simplification results in the reduction of circumstances and procedures in consideration of the "purposes" each element is meant to fulfill. Yet the simplification that results from reduction is not without aesthetic consequences, one category of which, for example, is minimalism.

MINIMAL SURFACES

Simple forms—including those that result from serial construction, the grid, repetitive patterns, and so on—have been important in recent avant-garde artistic practices. Rosalind Krauss has characterized repetition in the work of Donald Judd as an aesthetic alternative to the European formalism of relational art. The use of repetition in Judd's work was not a representation of rationalism but a simple statement of order, or how things happen "one after the other": "What is characteristic of the approach taken by the minimalist sculptors [Judd, Andre, Smithson, and Serra] is that they exploited a kind of found object for its possibilities as an element in a repetitive structure."[23] In her account of this idea, Krauss referred to its similarity to days following each other without anything giving them form, independent of their being inhabited and lived. An art of repetition, then, would be a way of finding out what the world is about, while its emphasis on continuities and intervals produced nonhierarchical structures. Works by these artists denied the task of using sculpture expressionistically. The idea was not to use sculpture to represent on the outside something of the work's inner essence, as had been the case with contemporary sculpture. The use of ready-made elements, such as bricks by Carl Andre, placed the emphasis on externality, reinforced by the use of mass-produced elements. The discussion of minimalism has corollaries in the use of cladding panels inasmuch as these panels are elements of mass production and can be used in ways that not only reinforce their associations with rationality but derive their significance from the specific circumstances of their arrangement and placement.

Proposals for an "anti-art" by minimalist artists also contributed to the postwar reconsideration of the relationship between artistic means and ends. Robert Morris, for example, argued for reduced distance between "form" and process: "I believe there are 'forms' to be found within the activity of making as much as within the end products."[24] Artistic activity is certainly intentional, but Morris did not accent its cognitive, deliberative, or ideational side, but rather its corporeal or bodily aspects. Each manner of making is a "structural mode of behavior," a kind of comportment, an attitude toward the world that discovers its patterns in an artist's encounters with specific materials, which might be better termed "kinds of resistance." More important than any of Pollock's "ideas" was the fact that he laid his canvases on the floor, allowing his back muscles, as much as gravity, to become "intentional" agents in artistic production. Morris writes, "The body's activity as it engages in manipulating various materials according to processes has open to it different possibilities of behavior." And as the means change, so do the ends. Each way of working is a "tendency," an inclination or likelihood that leads toward a certain "style" of outcomes. This was as true for Donatello as for Judd or for Morris himself. Moreover, the history of art, far from being a sequence of motifs or forms, is essentially a history of ways of making; hence its future: "for art to renew itself, it must go outside itself, stop playing with the given form and methods"; it must embark on new forms of conduct in concrete dialogue with the materials of the world. Accordingly, the making of a work will no longer involve arranging but building, not composing but constructing, and this constructing will involve materials that have never presented themselves to artists before; they will be materials arising out of new possibilities of manufacture and technology, including serial manufacture, such as Donald Judd exploited.

Such an art would not only be true to our time, completing what Morris described as "the secularization of art," but it would be "concrete." The vocabulary and concepts of concrete art arose well before Morris's arguments for an anti-art, and they arose outside the circles of American artistic practice, in Europe in fact, where these debates also had direct architectural consequences. The term "concrete art" arose in De Stijl circles in the teens. Shortly thereafter Theo van Doesburg inaugurated a journal called *Art Concret*. The buildings, paintings, and writings of Max Bill, however, are perhaps the best cases to consider, for one of the basic premises of his "concrete art" was the self-sufficiency of the means employed in artistic production. These means do not serve to depict anything; they constitute the work itself, even a work of architecture.

If art is expressive, Bill maintained, it is of the human spirit, not of something in "external" nature. Obviously, this view differs from the "corporeal" intentionality of later American minimalist production, but the resistance to "depiction" is the same in both cases, as is the faith in "automatic" procedures, "plastic mathematics," and the "materials themselves." Hans Frei, in his book on Bill, posed a basic question about the application of this artistic attitude to architecture: Can there be a *konkrete Architektur* when that practice must contend with so many nonartistic factors?[25] Were the answer to be yes, one would have to see some correspondence between the principles of concrete art and the characteristics of the buildings. Such a correspondence would involve reconciling the functional characteristics of the building with the aesthetic qualities of the art. That architecture can be seen in this way was suggested some time ago by Alfred Roth, whose commentary on Bill's Swiss Pavilion for the 1936 Milan Triennale invoked the concept of "free" forms and the autonomy or concreteness they presuppose. The pavilion, he said, "is an example of the practical utilization of the knowledge of constructive painting and plastics in conjunction with the new architecture."[26] This involved, he thought, "free arrangement" of architectural elements, "free forms," and "free colors," elements whose aesthetic or expressive qualities arose out of their material properties alone. That these forms and qualities were diverse and distinct did not prevent the setting in which they were placed from being uniform or harmonious; instead, the "construction" of rhythms and patterns was disciplined by the "mathematical" intelligence of the artist. Nor did the construction of free and diverse forms presume heterogeneity; throughout the building, elements and patterns repeated themselves, as if the unity and harmony of a work of concrete art depended on some measure of repetition.

Despite this, or perhaps in parallel with it, repetition has been understood differently in other examples of twentieth-century architecture, especially the sort that enthusiastically embraced mass production. It is well known that Le Corbusier praised industrial forms in America and used them as examples of his newly formed purist aesthetics and as a criticism of traditional (style) architecture. This same sensibility can be seen in the writings and projects of many other early modern architects and critics as well.[27] In these instances, repetition was not thought to be a matter of aesthetics but part of the project of rationalizing industrial production. These products did have aesthetic qualities, but they were assumed or argued to result from the (nonartistic) practices that brought them into being.[28] The early twentieth-century aesthetic of streamlined contours represents an indicative and instructive counterexample. Expression, in many instances, seems to have been "designed" in streamlining. The reverse was nevertheless also true; simplification in some solutions resulted from sheer pragmatism.

How, then, is architectural cladding to be understood: as aesthetic impulse or technological imperative? Is it, perhaps, both?

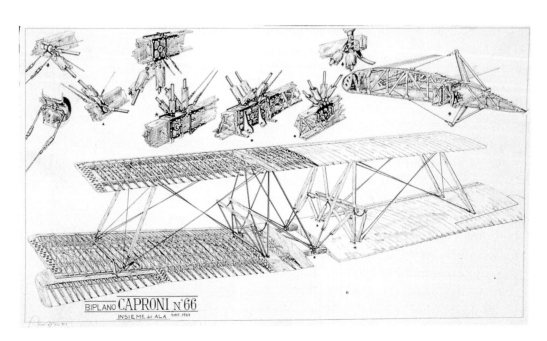

2.6
Caproni biplane bomber of composite construction in wood and metal, 1924.

2.7

Biplane, wing frame in steel with
adjustable lift wires, 1930.

THE FACTORY

The relationship between representation and construction in modern cladding inserts the logic of the factory into the center of the problem. This has no precedent in previous modes of production. In current building, the factory floor, workshop bench, and assembly table in part substitute for the role of the construction site in traditional building; it is in the factory, or the assembly shop, that the parts that make up buildings are produced. The mass production of windows, doors, and all types of coverings has resulted in construction becoming assembly, thereby redefining construction. A building's uniqueness results from the reconfiguration of premade and repetitive elements. The logic of repetitive production makes attunement to a specific climate and given place more difficult. Accordingly, architectural design must be redefined within the context of industrialized production. Design cannot rely solely on extending the logic of the factory into the site, nor can the uniqueness of a project neglect the imperatives of mass production. Avoiding this duality means developing a sense of building in tension with contemporary technology, one in which elements that are premade in the factory and workshop are remade in design and construction.

TOTAL CONTAINMENT

Cladding elements constitute a system that projects complete enclosure. The greatest achievement of this projection is perfect integrity of the system, which results from totality of containment. The best example would be the skin of an airplane. Yet the idea of a repetitive unbroken covering or uniform and continuous wrapping transforms the way the building skin mediates the inside and outside. How can the work of mediation be reconciled with the logic of a system of containment? Does cladding, as a system, deprive the exterior, the street or the city, of its role in developing the facade? How can an individual cladding panel as an element of construction allow for the sectional mediation that characterizes a facade? One possible answer involves attention to the "workings" of the facade: its operable windows, instruments of cooling or of lighting, and other mediations of site and climate. Yet the movement toward a total or complete container is hard to resist, given the premise of repetition brought about by both economic and aesthetic concerns. It may be that the problem is not with the idea of cladding as a container, nor even with its nature as a system, but with the manner and completeness of its closure. Cladding does not constitute the whole of an architectural facade; its panels, whether metal, concrete, or glass, are fixed to a structural frame, which is equally important in defining the limits of the building. The relationship between the two, however conceived, demonstrates the reconciliation of technology and appearance.

The problem of the relationship between a structural frame and a cladding system first became apparent in the early history of the structural frame as developed in a number of cities, but most notably in Chicago at the end of the nineteenth century.

CHICAGO FRAMES

Colin Rowe asserted that the frame developed in Chicago "is to modern architecture what the column was to classic architecture." In his account, not only is the frame the catalyst of modern architecture but it has even become modern architecture, appearing when not even structurally necessary.[29] In Chicago, however, the idea of supporting the whole of a multistory building on a skeletal frame did not first emerge in the minds of architects. Louis Sullivan wrote that "in Chicago the tall office building would seem to have arisen spontaneously, in response to favoring physical conditions, and the economic pressure as then sanctified, combined with the daring of promoters."[30]

The economic pressure to which Sullivan alluded was "the passion to sell," a passion felt by all Americans, the "impelling power in American life"; but in this case, it was a passion felt by the sales managers of eastern steel mills. These mills had for some time been manufacturing structural elements for use in bridge building. The salesmanship that brought the idea of the Chicago frame to the architects was based on the financial advantages of enclosing greater areas of office space in a rapidly growing city. Sullivan did not acknowledge, however, that an aesthetic of simplicity was also emerging at this time. Nevertheless, "the trick was turned; and there swiftly came into being something new under the sun."[31]

Claude Bragdon developed a similar argument: "Impelled by engineering skill and economic necessity, skyscraper architecture in America now seems to be on its way." Column and cornice decoration were discarded, to the advantage "not only of the pocket book" but also "of the optic nerve." In this passage, and in others, Bragdon did not ignore the aesthetics of simple construction; in his praise of Sullivan, of the frame, and in his philosophical aesthetics, "simple" is

2.8

Claude Bragdon, skyscrapers medieval
and modern, 1932.

equivalent to beautiful. The "bones" of these new frame buildings were what gave them their greatest beauty, their stark ornament needing "no veneer of constructed architectural ornament." "There is no need of culture during business hours."[32]

Although in Sullivan's account the tall building—not necessarily a skyscraper—had been shaped by practical and not aesthetic necessity, he was deeply committed to the development of ornament and to the apology for its use, as were his clients, who were not lacking in aesthetic judgment nor a sense of what was appropriate to different building types.[33] Sullivan's reputation among many of his contemporaries grew out of his work in architectural decoration. Bragdon, however, saw Sullivan's contribution otherwise: aesthetic good had resulted from concentration on new materials and new building methods, which gave rise to new architectural forms "in themselves." To support this, he cited Sullivan's belief that "it is of the very essence of every problem that it contains its own solution."[34] Ornament as the display of historical knowledge was rejected in skyscraper architecture, so that the building could be "well-formed and comely in the nude."[35] John Root argued similarly: "to every thoughtful man in Chicago [it is evident] that all conditions, climatic, atmospheric, commercial and social, demand for [the building's] external aspect the simplest and most straightforward expression."[36]

The aesthetic and functional development of the skeletal frame redefined the nature of walling in architecture. Deprived of ornament, and of load-bearing requirements, walling became "infill," a covering, container, or wrapper, hung behind, within, or in front of the open spaces of a frame. The status of walling as an "image" was thus redefined. For Sullivan, it is important to stress, this suppression of ornament was less an architectural end in itself than a training of the mind, a discipline of design that would reduce the likelihood of unnecessary ornament appearing in architecture. Chicago clients, however, were more doubtful about the necessity of surface ornament on all parts of all buildings: "businessmen [were] too wide awake for architects to try their tricks on them."[37]

Apart from the "passion" of these businessmen, contemporary conditions of production also influenced the development of the structural frame. In a broader cultural context, these conditions gave rise to questions about the relationship between early twentieth-century mass production or mechanization and artistic expression. How could individual expression be reconciled with systems of repetitive manufacture? This question, and others like it, were much debated in arts and crafts circles in both America and Europe. At the center of all of these debates, and the oppositions they elaborate, is the principle of simplification. Frank Lloyd Wright, for example, argued that simple surfaces were characteristic of the time because they were congenial to contemporary mechanized production. They were also key to his aesthetic. Is this by coincidence? If not, how can Wright's statements about simplicity be reconciled with his advocacy of "organic architecture," when that practice envisages each building as unique, insofar as each is built "from the ground up" and no two pieces of ground are alike? In advocating aesthetic simplicity, Wright followed William Morris, for whom, Wright claimed, this quality was as vital to the art of the machine as it was the basis of all true art. The aim was to have the design make the best of the "technical contrivances that produced them."[38] While this may seem to subordinate design to manufacture, both are ruled by the same principle: straight lines and squares made "as cunning as possible." This phrase had become the goal of both steel manufacture and surface design.

For Wright, the machine, "a normal tool of civilization," provided advantages over construction practices that relied on the reproduction of forms from other times—a construction practice that he thought had "murderous ubiquity" in his time. This prevalence represented a mistaken neglect of the conditions that give rise to forms in architecture. For the English as well as the American proponents of the arts and crafts movement, mechanization was accepted as a means of reducing the drudgery of manual labor, though it was clear that the machine should not be allowed to dominate "the workman and reduce his production to mechanical distortion."[39] The ideal of simplicity was "vital to the art of the machine," just as it was essential in Wright's aesthetic of rectilinearity; further, it allowed many to view handcraft as "distortion" and standardized machine form as "true art." This view easily accommodated the technical and aesthetic characteristics of the frame, but also those of its infill—the substitute for walling that would develop into cladding.

From the outset of the development of the frame in Chicago, architects struggled with the tension between representation of the wall, as an outmoded form of construction, and the frame as an outgrowth of contemporary production. This tension is apparent in the contrast between two buildings constructed in 1889: the Auditorium Building by Adler and Sullivan and the First Leiter Building by William Le Baron Jenney.

Adler and Sullivan's building, despite its programmatic inventiveness, creates its monumentality through associations with traditional modes of rusticated

2.9
Dankmar Adler and Louis Sullivan,
Auditorium Building, detail, Chicago,
1889.

walling. This is evident in the surface treatment of the wall as well as in its apparent depth. The use of an arcade on the middle levels also implies the existence of a load-bearing wall, suggesting arcuated not trabeated construction. The facade is also divided into horizontal layers according to the traditional distinction between base, middle, and top. This division further emphasizes the vertical dimension and reinforces the impression of the wall's structural autonomy. Evidence of the horizontal members of the structural frame, which are obviously coincident with the floor slabs, have been suppressed behind the profiles of the vertical members.

The equal significance of horizontal and vertical members—the tectonic integrity of the frame—is treated very differently in Jenney's First Leiter Building. Here the floors are supported by iron columns placed behind the masonry piers that subdivide the facade. As a result, the dimension of the piers is reduced and the size of the windows increased. While this combination of iron columns and masonry piers is not a genuine structural frame, it is significant because it involved no attempt to represent a load-bearing wall. To the contrary, what was emphasized were the points of intersection between the vertical and horizontal members, apparently denying the impact of gravity. Perhaps the distinction between wall and frame in the Auditorium and the First Leiter buildings is related to the distinction between a civic and a commercial structure—assuming that both architects designed their facades in consideration of expectations of facade treatment according to building type. Regardless of this qualification, the question remains about the correspondence between facade representation and construction in the new frame buildings. Facade design was also affected by the technical possibility of achieving high-rise construction—a possibility brought about by the increased load-bearing strength of the new materials. High-rise construction and the widespread use of glass in the intervals of the frame led to an overall uniformity of the entire surface of the facade. This uniformity was apparent in both tall buildings and early skyscrapers, and in both types frame infill became cladding, as is apparent in Louis Sullivan's later works.

Sullivan's Schlesinger and Mayer Store, later Carson Pirie Scott (1899–1904), limits the representation of the civic dimension of the building at street level to the vertical treatment of its corner entrance and its articulated and ornamented lowest two stories. At the upper levels, horizontal bands are widened and form an unbroken surface when they intersect with the narrower vertical members, giving the impression of a uniform surface—a flat plane—into which window openings have been punched. Because the windows have been placed

2.10
William Le Baron Jenney, First Leiter
Building, Chicago, 1879.

2.11
Louis Sullivan, Carson Pirie Scott
building, Chicago, 1904.

2.12
Detroit hotel, rear view,
from Erich Mendelsohn,
Amerika (1928).

behind the front surface of the frame, the construction preserves the impression of depth and of a solid wall. This impression also results from the traditional use of the windowsill, brought about by the necessity of acknowledging the weather: rain, wind, and snow acting on the surface of the building. The emphasis on the horizontal banding of the building also altered the proportions of the windows, making them more elongated. This shift toward a more horizontal window is also evident in Solon S. Beman's Studebaker building (1895) and in Holabird and Roche's McClurg building (1899–1900). Nevertheless, in many of these examples the larger and horizontal areas of glass are invariably interrupted by narrower vertical members. This anticipates the development of the ribbon window and later the widow wall, to which we will turn in the next chapter. These characteristic elements were later seized on by contemporary painters such as Edward Hopper as the most vivid and often melancholic images of twentieth-century life. Aside from art, however, the large expansive glass illuminated an expanded work area with its ensuing potential increase in profits and improvement in working conditions.

In none of the tall buildings built in Chicago during this period were the prominence and visual significance of the front facade questioned or reconsidered. Despite the emphasis on the buildings' volume, many retain a primary distinction between front and back. Ironically, it was the backs of many of these buildings that appeared to contemporary European architects as the "true expression" of the Chicago frame. This judgment is apparent in the selection of views in Erich Mendelsohn's *Amerika* and in Le Corbusier's comments in *When the Cathedrals Were White*.[40] In the backs there was little or no difficulty in reconciling the imperatives of representation with those of construction, because their external appearance was directly determined by the "facts" of building production, daylight requirements, and considerations of climate. This is a question not only of the presence or absence of ornament but of the representational possibilities of contemporary construction—production as representation.

In the Chicago frame buildings, the gradual increase in the size of the window challenged the traditional role of the wall with small openings. Though this increase in window size had been intended as a way of increasing the amount of light within the building, and therefore its rentable area, the proportional enlargement of the area of glass and in turn that of the window brought about a transformation of the wall itself, making the difference between the window and the wall ambiguous. Cladding history thus intersected with the history of the window.

Any seeing of an object by me is instantaneously repeated between all those objects in the world which are apprehended as co-existent, because each of them is all that the others "see" of it.
—Maurice Merleau-Ponty, *Phenomenology of Perception*

In front of a window seen from inside a room, I placed a painting representing exactly that portion of the landscape covered by the painting. Thus the tree in the picture hid the tree behind it, outside the room. For the spectator, it was both inside the room within the painting and outside in the real landscape. This is how we see the world. We see it outside of ourselves, and at the same time we only have a representation of it in ourselves.
—René Magritte, "Life Lines"

In contemporary architectural practice, the appearance of buildings largely results from the arrangement and assembly of premade products, a decisive instance of which is the selection of stock windows or glazing systems which give buildings their visual and formal characteristics. When one attempts to use the trade literature that advertises these products, one observes two kinds of information, aesthetic and technical, which give the architect a combined sense of unlimited freedom of choice, reliability, and improved performance. The emphasis on the window's function as a thermal barrier and light source has, indeed, led to advances in performance, but this emphasis has also had aesthetic consequences. For example, many manufacturers and architects select windows that preserve the form, shape, and look of traditional windows. Yet contemporary examples of the traditional sash window reveal variations in detail and function that result less

3.1
Bernasconi et al., Palazzo Olivetti,
Milan, 1955.

from aesthetic decisions than from performance requirements—variations such as mullions that are made thicker and heavier for the purpose of receiving two panes of glass (thermopane glazing) instead of one, or the use of snap-in plastic muntins on the surface of larger panes of glass. These changes in dimension have resulted in changes in proportion and have altered relationships commonly taken to be proper to a window's lineaments.

From the existing trade literature, one gets the impression that the aim is to "save appearances" and consequently save the traditional associations of these elements. In general, the emphasis is on preserving the image of the traditional window, rather than addressing the visual and aesthetic repercussions of technological advancements in window construction. Similarly, the interiors depicted in this literature often stereotype traditional ideals—whether domestic, professional, or industrial. But, given the current advances in window performance together with related changes in contemporary means of production, as well as doubts one might have about the acceptability of these stereotypes, assumptions about the need to save appearances should be reconsidered. Our aim in this chapter is to undertake this reconsideration, and to do so by reflecting on the meanings of the term "performance" when applied to an element such as the window.

DE-VIGNOLIZATION

Le Corbusier once claimed that the history of architecture was the same as the history of the window.[1] Before the twentieth century, he argued, architectural history had followed the development of the load-bearing wall punctured by apertures. Accordingly, the rules of this architecture were based on Vignola's codification during the Renaissance of the tenets of Greek and Roman art, then highly honored. Despite his admiration for the Acropolis, Le Corbusier found the idea of eternal rules for expressing "the nobility of the human spirit (the academic profession of faith)" to be false. Thus his proposal to "de-Vignolize" architecture was as much a reaction to the architectural limitations of these rules as it was to the persistent and widespread success of their contemporary practitioners—made more personally acute after the debacle of the League of Nations competition.

While "Vignola" had been concerned with the area between the windows, (walls, pilasters, and columns), Le Corbusier's "de-Vignolization" of architecture, combined with his affirmation of "architecture [as] lighted floors," proposed a treatment of the window as an element in itself. The introduction of the horizontal window as one of Le Corbusier and Jeanneret's "five points of a new architecture" was a reflection of their concentration on this element.[2] They argued that the regular perforations of the surface of the facade were the pure expression of a system of construction; when that system of construction changed, so should the expression. The use of steel and reinforced concrete led Le Corbusier to advocate the long, continuous, horizontal window, a window with no apparent limit, paralleling the landscape's horizon. Windows of this sort were imagined as part of a "free facade," two important aspects of which were its absence of supportive quality and its detachment from interior partitions. As such, the facade and horizontal windows had great geometric clarity and aesthetic significance. The result of allegiance to contemporary constructional possibilities was for Le Corbusier "spiritual enjoyment, [apparent in] proportions . . . thin verticals . . . unbroken surfaces . . . [serving as] the basis of architectural sensations."[3]

In *Precisions,* the horizontal window was presented as an instrument for increasing the amount of light in a building's interior. Accenting another kind of performance, in *The Radiant City* Le Corbusier celebrated the glass wall as the "lungs" of the building.[4] Horizontal glazing was also a device for joining the room to the landscape, particularly when the latter was conceived as an extended horizon. Through this instrument the landscape and the building were both sited and sighted. In *Une petite maison,* for example, the building's siting resulted from placing a viewpoint in the landscape (geographically and topographically), and this viewpoint was focused through the horizontal window.[5] Plan and plot were joined through view: "In my pocket was the plan of a house. A plan without a site? The plan of a house in search of a plot of ground? Yes! [The location] offers an unparalleled view, which cannot be spoiled by building, [a view] of one of the finest horizons in the world . . . the plan is tried out on the site and fits it like a glove."[6] The house as an instrument for "survey of" is permanently "sited within" the landscape. Thus the window's sheet of glass is self-reflexive; in it and through it, landscape and building collapse into a spatial and visual slippage in which reciprocating views make a continuous horizon.

Le Corbusier broadened this principle in later writings and projects. In *Precisions,* for example, horizon is all-inclusive, making prospect equivalent to nature; hence the striking formula: "composition: geometry + nature = humanity."[7] This formula served as a commentary on a set of images in which

3.2
Le Corbusier, horizontal window from
Une petite maison (1954).

windows demonstrating different construction techniques were also capable of joining parts of the landscape together: foreground, roads, and trees with background mountains. This joining was neither direct nor traditional, however. With the vertical window, the connections between inside and outside were naturalized in at least two ways: (1) by paralleling the form of the window with the upright posture of the viewer's body, and (2) by instituting an inhabitable space in the thickness of the window wall, making an experiential threshold between street and room.[8] The horizontal window, on the contrary, instituted a virtual connection and a physical separation between landscape and interior; its thin glass plane served as a mechanism for framing the panorama of nature, rendering it artificial on and through the surface of the ribbon window. The window as an element of separation formed a distance across which connection assumed recollection, or joining presumed memory, so constituting a horizon of yearning.[9]

The building's structure played a particular role in this horizon. Le Corbusier's large buildings of the 1930s developed different variations on the free facade, windows, and load-bearing columns. In the Salvation Army building, for example, concrete columns are recessed behind the front glass plane and the edges of the slabs are tapered, seemingly to escape notice. The load-bearing elements of the Swiss Pavilion, however, approach the outer surface and engage the primary divisions of the window just behind or beneath its surface, rather like the recesses behind the glass plane but also interrupted by the outer edge of the floor slab. The Clarté apartment building represents a third alternative; structural steel columns are coincident with the building's outer surface, in both plan and section. Horizontal ribbon windows, like those developed in the little house on Lake Geneva, still exist on the facade of this third case, but with an important difference. In the Clarté apartments, the stratification of a lower, middle, and upper part of the interior wall is achieved by distinctions between transparent and translucent glass, rather than between solid wall and glass. The transparent surface forms the middle level, which is also the largest and becomes the horizon of viewing. The result of this new treatment of the wall is that two different readings are possible: on the outside the glass wall reads as a continuous surface, and on the inside as an interior horizon. The continuity of surface on the exterior results from the sameness of material (glass) in much of the facade, but also from the regular subdivisions of its parts, fully coincident and coplanar with the intervals of the structural frame. From the apartment interiors, no such comprehensive view is possible; each unit is planned with its long dimension perpendicular

3.3
Le Corbusier and Pierre Jeanneret,
Swiss Pavilion, Cité Universitaire,
Paris, 1932.

to the facade, reducing the linear and horizontal dimension (in contrast to the house on Lake Geneva) and making the interior horizon coordinate with the space of the room. The external balconies extend the space of the room into the exterior, as they subdivide the surface of the facade. Their purposes are many: (1) providing an external room for the apartments, (2) serving as sunscreens on the south side of the building, (3) recalling the typology of local apartment buildings, (4) acting as a permanent scaffolding during construction and after for maintenance, and (5) dividing the facade into two-story units that correspond to the structure of the apartments. As such, these balconies acknowledge the purposes fulfilled by apertures in traditional (thick) wall construction but in this case with thin, lightweight, and industrialized elements. Ironically, this incorporates aspects of the vertical window into its opposite; inhabitable space has been reinterpreted through an assembly of lightweight elements. This "wall" can be seen as infill, window wall, and uniform plane.

VIEWING THE LANDSCAPE

The images of the Clarté building that Le Corbusier published in his *Oeuvre complète* illustrate views through the interior and beyond the balcony, into an open landscape.[10] This type of view recurred in his photographs and drawings; it can be seen in the drawings of the Wanner apartments, the *petite maison* on Lake Geneva, the Villa Cook, and many other projects. Even in the views of his own apartment interior, on Rue Nungesser-et-Coli, this type was significant.[11] In very few of these photographs, however, is the immediate adjacency of neighboring buildings apparent; nor, for that matter, is the urban situation. Instead, Le Corbusier develops a photographic version of landscape painting.

A very simple but indicative drawing published in Jules Alazard and Jean-Pierre Herbert's *De la fenêtre au pan de verre dans l'oeuvre de Le Corbusier* represents a window wall made up of its key elements: an outline frame, a horizon, and verticals. While clearly a window, this also appears to be a canvas or a tableau onto which a landscape is displayed, at least a landscape reduced to its representative elements. The figures rendered in this landscape are as few as the lineaments that divide the composition, but they are just as significant. In the middle ground are a modulor man, trees, and the sun. The traditional division of prospect into foreground, middle ground, and background is condensed in this image onto the flat surface of the window/canvas by means of the horizontal and vertical glazing

3.4
Le Corbusier, Clarté apartments,
Geneva, 1932.

3.5
Le Corbusier, Clarté apartments,
balcony, Geneva, 1932.

3.6

Le Corbusier, window wall, 1932,
from Alazard and Herbert, *De la fenêtre
au pan de verre dans l'oeuvre de Le
Corbusier* (1933).

bars, which act as regulating lines on the "canvas" and horizon lines in the landscape. This condensed image is less an interpenetration of inside and outside than an arrangement of lines that denaturalize the landscape by appropriating it into the regulating geometry of the painter's (modulor) eye, thus merging window construction with landscape composition. Pages of *The Modulor* illustrate the applicability of this geometry to buildings, their details, and landscapes, once again condensing the whole into a regular pattern. Modulor geometry governs buildings and landscapes, establishing a law of composition and of perception. Quite apart from its subdivisions, the horizontal frame of this window carries associations with landscape paintings, suggesting landscape siting even when it is located within an urban context. This contradiction between the landscape and the urban condition is, perhaps, most evident in one of Le Corbusier's drawings of the interiors of the Wanner apartments in Geneva, where the view of the suspended garden shows distant hills and a landscape devoid of inhabitation, despite the density of the existing block arrangement and the building's proximity to others.

The use of the horizontal window in Le Corbusier's architecture suggests that this contradiction between intended horizon and existing context can be generalized for much of modern architecture: contrary to what drawings such as this aspire to, the vision of an unlimited natural vista has rarely been achieved in the dense urban projects of modern architecture.[12] In America, for example, many social housing projects utilized the picture window on the ground level as if they were facing a landscape, yet this urban space was hardly pastoral and in fact became, in far too many cases, something of a war zone. Above this level, however, openings onto "nature" allowed for uncontrolled gazing into neighboring windows—which Magritte illustrated ironically in *Eloge de la dialectique* and Alfred Hitchcock portrayed dramatically in *Rear Window,* showing nearby openings as the site of a revealing plot.

One unintended result of the use of the "Corbusian" horizontal window in dense urban settings is that conventional ideas about openness and visibility have been called into question. When the natural landscape is replaced by the urban, the window as a place for viewing out becomes also the place where others peer in. The transformation of the singular (outward) view into potentially reciprocating views (looking at and being looked at) thus destabilized conventional understandings of the function of windows. In films like Hitchcock's, this situation prompted voyeuristic experiences ranging from titillation to intrigue to surveillance.

OPACITY AND TRANSPARENCY

The potential richness of this dialectical urban situation is apparent in paintings contemporary with Le Corbusier's designs, especially those by Raoul Dufy and Henri Matisse. Dufy's *The Studio in the Impasse de Guelma,* for example, consists of a doubling or multiplication of windows, such that the division between inside and outside is made unclear. Through an open door, in the depth of the interior space, an arrangement of paintings mainly depicting seascapes reflects the appearance of a window. In the middle of the room, behind a foreground canvas, a large window opens onto the upper horizon of an urban scene. Unlike images that simply and unambiguously distinguish inside from outside, Dufy's painting disturbs conventions by exchanging near for far and inviting the viewer to remake topographical distance according to clues of pictorial construction. Rather than recognizing something familiar, we witness the advent of a situation we participate in making.[13] The painting does not represent a conventional situation but proposes one to be constructed. It is pointless to debate the modernity of this image; what matters instead is the openness of the situation.[14] One could find beneath the objects that fill the space of Dufy's painting the regulating geometry of Le Corbusier's wall window, but, in the absence of the pure "natural" landscape of Le Corbusier, Dufy's landscapes build up a spatial situation as much through transparency as through opacity. This opacity is built up by coordinating all of the things relevant to the situation, akin to a stage set and its "props." Not empty though, nor a space through which vision and action can freely pass, this is a set or setting that is *thickened* by relationships among things, whereby they cover and uncover themselves, each occluding the edge of the other, making points into the distance virtually continuous. In pictorial composition this transforms the window of perspective into a field or horizon of practical affairs.

Even greater opacity exists in the window scenes painted by Matisse.[15] Unlike Dufy, Matisse builds up the density of the image by planes or fields of color and pattern rather than the coordination of "props." The result, however, is the same: a spatial situation in which exterior and interior develop new, or nonperspectival, relationships of coordination and interpenetration. Consider, for

3.7

Raoul Dufy, *The Studio in the Impasse de Guelma*, 1935.

example, Matisse's *Red Interior: Still Life on a Blue Table*. The dominant color and pattern spread themselves across the floor, up the walls, and outside the door/window into the garden without gradation of color intensity or interruption of pattern. Although the absence of conventional perspectival depth flattens the space of the image, the red zigzag joins the parts of the scene together as one "horizon." The blue of the foreground table and the green of the background trees strengthen the unity of the red middle ground by providing strong contrast. The window, which in conventional constructions is viewed as an instance of spatial division, is, in the midst of this expansive red pattern, an instrument for upturning the outdoor terrace, causing the garden itself to advance frontally toward the plane of the tabletop flowers, thereby exchanging its far for a near position—as if the flowers have been returned to the place from which they were taken. Spatial depth is also flattened by the foreground table, which is more or less circular in shape, as if it had been turned so that its top side faces front, not its front edge; the same is true for the apples. Because the space of the room is so thin, the window allows the viewer to variously merge and separate the landscape and the interior. While different from Dufy's painting, Matisse's image likewise allows us to reimagine the nature of the window as an instrument of spatial separation. Rethinking the window in representation leads to reconsidering the "view" or "look" of its setting. This perspective, as a way of seeing settings of this kind, is both a graphic construction and a way of constructing reality through representation.[16] These paintings disavow perspective construction, or at least challenge it, and in so doing serve as the basis for a different construction of reality—at least the reality of residing at the edge of an interior. Linear perspective is not neglected in this challenge but is rediscovered as a topic of seeing, understanding, and imagining the interior and the exterior landscape.

The *locus classicus* of discussions about the early construction of perspectival depth is the drawing by Albrecht Dürer illustrating the construction of a perspective drawing.[17] In this well-known image, the space between the male painter and the female model is interrupted by a grill, which intersects the cone of vision at right angles. The grill is duplicated on the artist's panel and with it the three-dimensional figure of the model depicted in two dimensions. The frontal view Dürer has constructed for us is at right angles to the painter's cone of vision. If our view is legitimate and conventional, the painter's view of the reclining figure is hardly so. Both, however, make up this window scene. The monocular correspondence between what is seen through the grill and what is drawn on the artist's panel also fixes the "correct" position from which the drawing has to be viewed. From a different and therefore "incorrect" vantage point, another subject would be seen; one obviously irregular in the space of "legitimate constructions," but also, and perhaps because of its illegitimacy, one that could be seen as open and suggestive of other (and new) constructions.

THE OBLIQUE

The perspective frame is productive, then, in two ways: it produces affirmative constructions when used correctly, and it produces aberrations when used obliquely. A preference for the first sort of fiction cannot be sustained—even if thought desirable—because changed vantage points reveal different realities. This was demonstrated in anamorphic constructions from the time of Leonardo onward.[18] These sorts of images emerged in the faithful pursuit of legitimate constructions as an attempt to compensate for distortion resulting from viewing distances that were too short or too long.[19] In anamorphic projection, the figure's outlines are projected beyond themselves so that when viewed frontally they exhibit distortion, so much so that they become virtually unrecognizable. Only when seen obliquely, matching the viewpoint with the point of the (visual) pyramid, does the figure appear correctly. Frontal distortion dislocates viewing, thereby instituting a space between two constructions (the frontal and oblique). The spectator is invited to imagine a view that appears at the margins of the one presently seen. This provides the viewer with the opportunity to imagine contents in the deformed image—bringing forth the recognizable (hills, horses, houses) out of the incomprehensible—together with the possibility of selecting the "correct" view at the margins, which carries within itself traces of the former ("incomprehensible") view. True, correct, and proper in this sort of viewing are always probable, denying fixed and monocular frontality.

Some architects have recognized and utilized the opportunities of oblique views. Alvar Aalto's Baker House (1947–1948) at MIT is an example of a building that inscribes the oblique view. In an effort to escape, as much as possible, the disturbing prospect onto a street with heavy traffic, the facade of the building was curved in plan, avoiding where sensible the placement of windows parallel to the street. Preferred instead was a diagonal line of sight, as in the case of the view onto the landscape from the windows of a moving train.[20] Aalto's windows at Baker House are orchestrated so that they form a field that acts in conjunction

3.8
Alvar Aalto, Baker House,
Massachusetts Institute of Technology,
Cambridge, 1949.

with the building's curving wall. The field of the windows and the curve of the wall decelerate the speed of moving objects on the street by expanding the limits of the visible horizon across which objects move. The windows used in this building are conventional, but their oblique placement on the site modifies both the building and the city—the way it is made and is discovered.

Diagonal views also appear in De Stijl architecture, as a result of "centrifugal" plan composition.[21] In Gerrit Rietveld's Schroeder house, for example, the main points of van Doesburg's "Plastic Architecture" have been realized; it is anticubic, dynamic, and "transformable" in its plan and elements. The windows in the living room of this house occupy the corner of the plan. When they are closed, they conform to the planar, frontal composition that assumes a frontal view, as do the other windows in the house. When they are open, the corner disappears, allowing an oblique view of the landscape and denying their frontality. Furthermore, their placement perpendicular to the facade when open suggests sectional views, extending and destabilizing the virtual limits of the house. This is particularly evident from the balcony, where the open window allows an unexpected view of the landscape from a vantage point within it. In all of this the window serves as the prop for discovering new and unexpected relationships between the inside and outside.

This window, like any other, relies on mechanisms of operation, instruments of opening and closure. As props, these devices also set up one's sense of the way the building will perform. In modern architecture, the picture window opened the interior onto the exterior, but it also, and perhaps as a consequence, led to the development of new devices of enclosure, both moving and fixed. Replacing and reinterpreting traditional elements such as the curtain and shutters were rolling and concealable blinds, as well as sunscreens and different types of glass. These elements allowed for the adjustment of relationships between the interior and exterior, serving as props of performance, not only in the technical or functional sense of (thermal) performance, leading to comfort, but also as the indispensable props of the building's situational performance.[22]

Examples such as Baker House or the Schroeder house change the role of the window from a device limited to looking "at" the panorama to one that also includes the making of the building itself—its siting, plan, and section. In these buildings the window performs a function in excess of pictorial visuality. While both window types still prioritize seeing from inside to outside, these examples

3.9
Gerrit Rietveld, Schroeder house,
Utrecht, 1924.

delay the immediate appearance of the "natural" landscape, which was at the heart of the purified and "hygienic" terrains of Le Corbusier's urbanism.

THE PAINTED VIEW

The connection between the horizontal window and the landscape was further reinforced through the proportional similarities between these windows and the elongated horizontal frames used in paintings of landscape. Historically, much of landscape painting has been reaffirmative, utilizing and representing the social stability associated with nature and the countryside. Seen this way, the horizontal window as "framed landscape" can also be understood as a perpetuation of the morality of the nineteenth century—especially in that century's opposition to the congested and polluted city. In addition, there are many direct links between the depiction of idyllic nature in nineteenth-century French paintings, for example, and the figure of the rural working mother "as elemental, untutored—hence eminently 'natural' female—[and] the ideal signified for the notion of beneficent maternity."[23] The allegories of woman as nature in Western art have led to the literal juxtaposition of one with the other. According to C. M. Armstrong, "the female nude, when free of narrative situations, is most often constituted frontally and horizontally—as a kind of landscape, its significant part the torso, its limbs merely elongations of the line created by the supine, stretched out torso."[24] The associations between nature and the female body were also explored by Le Corbusier. In a series of drawings dating from 1932, one can see the direct reciprocities between what he saw as nature and the feminine. In one drawing there is a tree that can also be read as a voluptuous woman; in a later painting, *Nu féminin allongé et femme allongée au livre,* a reclining woman is directly juxtaposed with the landscape. Similar images exist in other works, especially the *Poem to the Right Angle.* In all of these images, "landscape" and the female merge as "nature."

THE DEPTH OF THE WINDOW WALL

All frames have depth, whether horizontal or vertical. For the frame of the window, and especially in modern windows, depth is of great importance. One might argue that Le Corbusier's development of the *brise-soleil,* the sun-breaking device for creating shade and shadow within the facade, also led to the denial of the frontality of the facade, creating an "in-between" spatiality belonging as

3.10

Le Corbusier,

Nu féminin allongé et femme allongée au livre, 1936.

3.11
Le Corbusier,
Carpenter Center for the Visual Arts,
Harvard University, Cambridge, 1963.

much to the inside as to the outside. Other props of this sort, such as *ondulatoires* or sun shades for the adjustment of light and view, have their equivalents in traditional windows, such as the ingenious designs of the Renaissance window, with its attention to transparency and ventilation as well as its devices for the control of light intensity (blinds, curtains, louvered shutters, etc.). The depth of the frame, in both modern and traditional windows, is as much a space of "adjustment" as it is of view; that is, while it is something seen and seen through, it is also an instrument that simultaneously connects and changes opposite situations. This makes it both passive and active: a receptacle, like the human eye, but also a tool, like a person's hand. The instrumental or handy nature of the window is often suppressed for the sake of general appearances.

TAKING STOCK

The contemporary residential stock window incorporates many technical advances. For example, it is relatively maintenance free, has a higher U value than traditional windows, and has better sealing details. It has also benefited from designs developed in the industrial and commercial sector. Nevertheless, in the United States there has been little design collaboration between residential and commercial manufacturers, in part because of specialization and differing economies of development. As a result, the residential market has been dominated by manufacturers of wood windows who see the reduction of cost and technical improvement as their main task. Less attention has been paid to the reexamination of these windows, especially their profile but also their use in a series to form a window wall. We have already observed the tendency to "save appearances" in the design and selection of these windows. The use of different types of wood trim to cover up the connections between the premade window and the rough opening also, if inadvertently, reinforces the traditional look of stock windows. Concentration on technical performance in window manufacture has taken for granted aesthetic performance but also, and perhaps more importantly, has taken for granted, or not explored, the window's *situational* performance. The architecture inscribed in the stock window requires certain details that often preclude the possibility of its use.

Contemporary window manufacturers try to illustrate aesthetic, technical, and situational performance in their marketing literature. Performance in each of these senses is measured against an assumed sense of what is proper. The question one should ask of this literature is how this suitability is understood, especially in view of the nature of the window as something that can be adjusted. Most stock windows marketed and sold today reaffirm the traditional look, creating a sense of authenticity through appearances. Performance in such an "authentic" situation amounts to the *virtual* reenactment of a routine that is taken to be certain and correct, at least visually so, because it equates "look" with social action. But this kind of reenactment is neither contemporary nor particular, let alone emancipatory.

BORDER ADJUSTMENTS

We have seen that the window is not only an instrument of seeing, or establishing the look of a building; it is also an instrument of adjustment: not only an "eye" but a "hand." When the window's parts—its shades, curtains, shutters, sashes—are moved, the room or settings in which it is placed also changes. These changes are apparent in lighting, temperature, noise, and other qualities that characterize and define the setting. Qualities such as these are not essentially visual; nonetheless, they contribute to the *construction* of the setting's character. Character in this sense is the outcome of the relationship between the social practice of the situation and one of the instruments of its definition.

The same reciprocity exists when considering the building's exterior. The window reframes the exterior at the same time as it remakes the interior. We have seen this already in the case of Le Corbusier's landscape drawings and the paintings of both Dufy and Matisse: the window is both passive and active, a receptacle and an instrument. If marginal (to the exterior view or qualities of interior light), it is also productive, "coming against, beside, and in addition [to the work done], not falling to one side, it touches and cooperates within the operation, from a certain outside . . . like an accessory that one is obliged to welcome on the border, on board [au bord, à bord]."[15] Oblique and anamorphic views had the same consequences.

Accordingly, a ready-made or stock window, whether traditional or modern, is not necessarily "incorrect" in itself. When diverted from the context of its visual (and at times the fixity of its historical) "authenticity," the stock window can be replaced/misplaced into new spatial situations that allow it to "adjust" or construct alternative frameworks for contemporary social practice. As a matter of built fact, this adjustment occurs in the space of tension between the window itself and its field, the wall, at the border of the building and its sites/sights. Accordingly, the choice does not lie solely in the selection of a modern horizontal or traditional stock window, but rather in the specific and situational modifications that are made to a window's lineaments as part of a constructed location, in order to inscribe architecture with the effects of its particular and circumstantial properties.

VERTICAL AND HORIZONTAL

The correspondence between aesthetic quality and technical possibility is similar to the case of the frame buildings in Chicago; there, too, production led to representation, in particular that of the backs of the buildings. When these frame buildings rose above the heights of traditional buildings, they had a uniformity of skin treatment on all sides, making them objectlike or volumetric. Le Corbusier also argued for a direct correspondence between systems of construction and representation on all sides of a building, although he did differentiate fronts from backs, as in the Salvation Army building, the Swiss Pavilion, and many of his houses, most notably the Villa Stein in Garches. And he did "compose" facades. In this, his stance can be distinguished from the position adopted by Auguste Perret, with whom he quarreled about the qualities of vertical and horizontal openings.[26] Apart from their debates about the quality and quantity of light in the interior, Perret observed that Le Corbusier's intention was primarily aesthetic; this was, he thought, the only conceivable rationale for his "torture" of the windows—their exaggerated lengths and reduced heights. Le Corbusier's purpose, Perret observed, was either decorative or to give the impression of volume. Certainly the exterior compositional geometry of the free facade was important to Le Corbusier, but equally so were some of its other qualities: flatness, lightness, and thinness. Mass-produced elements, which Le Corbusier praised often and insistently, also had these qualities. And obviously, they were produced repetitively, too.

In his rejection of Perret's vertical window, Le Corbusier overstated its traditional character. Indeed, windows of this kind, the kind that linked street, garden, and sky, had existed for centuries. But Perret himself interpreted and transformed this type. While in continuity with the anonymous tradition of Parisian urban architecture and reminiscent of the openings in neighboring buildings, his windows, like the wall into which they were placed, also acknowledged the possibilities of a new structural rationality. The windows of his apartment building on Rue Franklin (1903) are surrounded by a framework of post and lintel construction that brings to the surface the building's concrete structure.[27] No longer a display of decorative motifs on a masklike surface, opened only by "punched" windows, the facade has become the site of an interplay between frame, window, and panel, in which depth is achieved by the spatial carving of volumes within the facade bay by recesses in its central bay. Frame and panel are sharply distinguished, too: contrasted with the smooth and flat planarity of the frame's cladding are the mosaic-faced panels, which have for their surface a compacted depth or sedimented thickness juxtaposed to the smooth qualities of the frame. In Perret's Rue Raynouard apartment buildings (1929–1932) the vertical windows remain, but the strong contrast between frame and panel has been reduced as a result of the similar color and finish of the materials—concrete frame and stone panels. As a consequence, the facade is more planar and the panel appears more like infill. This effect is especially evident on the back facade, where the play of volumes gives way to a flat surface. The alignment between surface and structure on this facade achieves the correspondence between building production and facade articulation that Le Corbusier advocated, as well as an increase in window area, even with vertical windows. While they are typically urban and Parisian, Perret's facades are also able to achieve entirely modern effects, in that they admit more light than traditional types and modify their appearance through new construction methods. More significant than differences between the vertical and horizontal orientation of their windows is the fact that both Le Corbusier and Perret reinvented the wall and its windows; the first by rejecting the figurative or anthropomorphic tradition, and the second by transforming it.

MISALIGNMENTS

The play between vertical and horizontal within a composition of frame, panel, and window was central to the work of Giovanni Muzio in the 1930s, such as his apartment buildings on Piazza della Repubblica in Milan. The Palazzo Bonaiti, the largest of these two buildings, can be seen as an example of the palazzo type, demonstrating compositional geometry through the use of surface ornaments, particularly pilasters and entablatures.[28] Both the load-bearing elements and the infill cladding are built out of brick. The distinction between frame and panel, which was reduced in Perret's Rue Raynouard, is in this case reduced

3.12
Auguste Perret,
55 Rue Raynouard, Paris, 1932.
Photo: Charles H. Tashima, 1991.

even further through the use of one material for purposes that could be seen as opposites. Furthermore, the composition of the facade lacks the categorical distinction between vertical and horizontal elements observed in the buildings of Le Corbusier and Perret, showing instead an intermixing or combining of elements in the horizontal balconies with their vertical openings and recessed horizontal surface banding. Even though a structural frame appears across the face of the building, in certain places, such as the entryways, there is a misalignment between the expressed and the structural frame. On the upper levels a clear distinction between walling on the exterior and structure on the interior is apparent; what appears on the outside as the structural frame *represents* the actual load-bearing elements hidden within, but corrected. This use of "structure" as image also makes the "infill" panel ambiguous: it is both integral with a wall and contained within a frame, which also means it is both heavy and lightweight. This hiding and revealing of the frame in Muzio's Palazzo is, then, distinct from Perret's use of the frame as the necessary expression of built form. For this reason also, Muzio's building can be seen as an attempt to reconcile the modern use of the structural frame with the traditional use of the classical orders.[29]

Misalignment between the openings and intervals of a structural frame is also apparent in Adolf Loos's building on Michaelerplatz, Vienna (1909–1911). This building has, in fact, given rise to considerable debate and confusion about "rational" building, or the conformity between structure and appearance.[30] As in the example from Muzio, the structural frame in the Looshaus is variously hidden and revealed; not, however, in all parts of the facade but according to its three main levels: entry, mezzanine, and residential floors. Behind the facade's surface is a load-bearing concrete frame. The regularity of this frame is interrupted at the height of the mezzanine floor by an exposed beam—steel clad in copper—that transfers the load of the middle bays to the wide piers at either end. The striking fact about this beam—itself an emblem of modern industrial production, precedent for which can be found in William Le Baron Jenney's Manhattan Building in Chicago (1889)—is that it *appears* on the surface of the building; it coincides, in fact, with the capitals of the Doric order that defines the entry. The main part of the building's load-bearing structure, its concrete frame, is by contrast buried within or disassociated from the surface. Further, the entry-level Doric columns are non-load-bearing, for they arrived at the site after the frame had been completed and were inserted into the structural system, not as a supportive part but rather hung from the structure. While the columns may not

3.13
Adolf Loos, Goldman & Salatsch store
(Looshaus), Vienna, 1911.
Photo: Charles H. Tashima, 1991.

belong to the structural system, they do have a place on the site, as Czech and Mistelbauer have shown, marking the building's threshold and imitating the entry porch to Michaelerkirche. In a contemporary cartoon, with Fischer von Erlach in the foreground, yet another aspect of the facade is shown: its modernity, revealed in punched windows, large open expanses without columns, and flat un-ornamented surfaces. The fact that the building was hotly debated during its construction attests that it represented to Loos's contemporaries a break with tradition, while the use of the facade as a catalyst for the redefinition of the context shows Loos's willingness to hide the building's modernity. As a consequence, the facade is neither modern nor traditional, presenting a selectively exposed frame and a wall. What appears of the frame is contained within the wall. The same distinctions exist among the entry-level picture windows, mezzanine-level bay windows, and residential-level punched windows. Unlike in what exists of the frame in Perret's buildings, no comprehensive or total visual rationality of structural form is attempted here; instead, parts have *local or situated rationality:* the civility of the street entry, the serviceable appropriateness of the mezzanine with daylighting provided by the translucent wall of the tailor's workshop, the typically framed domesticity of the apartments, and the "modernity" of the roof. The building's windows, like its "cladding," situate it in its location.

CLADDING AS CLOTHING

It was within a horizon of social practice and urban experience—the city—that the Looshaus facade was developed, making it both unique as an object with various and particular parts and at the same time commonplace or anonymous, in conformity to an idea of Viennese architecture. Loos expressed his ideas about facade cladding in his commentary on clothing: "To be dressed correctly . . . is to be dressed in such a way that one stands out the least."[31] This statement bases aesthetic judgment on commonplace cultural interests and social practices: the dressing of an individual is identified or contrasted with the dressing of the collective. This premise generalizes the idea of the "commonplace"; in fact, the "everyday" to which Loos referred was not widely shared in Vienna or any other city—not even in London, which for Loos was the center of contemporary culture. What he hoped would be "unnoticed" was really less "common" than middle-class, especially the dress of the English gentleman, which was itself conservative. Restating the point about anonymity more exactly, Loos wrote: "An article of clothing is modern when the wearer stands out as little as possible at the center of culture, on a specific occasion, in the best society. This is a very English axiom, to which every fashionable intellectual would probably agree."[32] Nevertheless, propriety in architecture as in fashion depended also on location; the plain white surface treatment of the upper floors of the Looshaus belonged in Vienna because, Loos argued, "Vienna is a limewash city."[33] The difficulty of this assertion arose out of the fact that the Vienna to which he referred had been forgotten or neglected in the contemporary devotion to (non-Viennese) "style architecture," the Ringstrasse culture and the "elaborate emptiness" of the dying Hapsburg rule. Loos's "limewash" Vienna was something he imagined or idealized—even remythologized. There is thus a tension between his recognition of anonymous collective forms (of dressing or cladding) and self-conscious presentation of individual forms (dandyism). These concerns are paralleled by the ideas of the poet Georg Trakl, who during the years of this controversy abandoned the age-old dedication to the question "Who am I?" by replying "I am not!"—a reply similar to Rimbaud's comment, the "I is someone else."[34] Each of these quotations questions the individuality of the person or building, perhaps even destroys the expression of individuality, as a result of the "rational derangement of the senses."

The use of ornament as an end in itself had become pervasive in Hapsburg culture. The Viennese were not "well dressed"; they were "beautifully dressed." Karl Kraus wrote: "The streets of Vienna are paved with culture, the streets of other cities with asphalt."[35] In a similar vein, Egon Friedell wrote: "every material used tries to look like more than it is. Whitewashed tin masquerades as marble, papier mache as rosewood, plaster as gleaming alabaster, glass as costly onyx. . . . The butter knife is a Turkish dagger, the ash tray a Prussian helmet, the umbrella stand a knight in armor, and the thermometer a pistol."[36] In response to this excess, Loos stressed the material substance of ornament, the fact that ornament has a "material cause." This is evident in his rhetorical complaint: "If the leadership in clothing were left to the Viennese, sheep's wool would be woven to look like velvet and satin. Even though it is only made of wool, English clothing material, and thus our clothing material, never manifests the Viennese 'I'd really like it but can't afford it.' . . . Which brings us to the principle of cladding."[37] Material value is not in the material itself, but in the labor necessary for its formation. For Loos, all materials were of equal value. His "law of cladding" prohibited the confusion of a material clad with its cladding, and also prohibited the use of paper, paint, cloth, and other surfacing materials to represent materials other than themselves. Paper should not be made to look like brick or stone, and woven underclothes should not be dyed skin color. If a material looks like anything, it looks like itself: no material should claim for itself the form of another.

This understanding of materials explains another aspect of the Looshaus facade. The use of whitewash for the upper part of the building is as much a reference to the buildings of Vienna as it is a representation of the logic of construction inherent in the material's language. Forms in architecture arise out of the production methods and applications of materials, having come into being "with and through materials."[38] With typical irony, Loos observed that the best way to invent a saddle is to remain ignorant of leather and the way it is cut and sewn.[39] This fact of material formation is also true for a wide range of architectural materials: not only thick and palpable materials, such as stone, timber, and metals, but also thin and liquid coverings, such as stains and paints. All of the materials of the Looshaus facade—the stucco, marble, steel, glass, and copper—should be interpreted in this way, for each has its own language and method. The application of paint to the surface of another material is also conditioned by this same rule of propriety disallowing the imitation of another material. Accordingly, metal can be painted any color but a metallic color. The use of cladding in the Looshaus, then, should be understood as a result of three sorts of criteria: the requirements of the interior settings, those of the street or urban situation, and the practices of the craftsmen who built the building by shaping its materials.

But to accent materials and methods of construction would be to distort the interplay of issues at work in the making of this facade. The windows of the building, particularly those at the mezzanine level, can also be understood to represent Viennese culture insofar as they accommodate the practices that typify that culture. For this reason, equal emphasis should be placed on what we have called the situational performance of architectural elements, not only on the appearance of their tectonic performance or their similarity or dissimilarity to antecedents.

Several historians have discussed similarities between these apertures and examples in Chicago commercial architecture. For example, in their study of the Looshaus Czech and Mistelbauer pointed to Burnham and Root's Rookery (1886).[40] By this time the bay window had become commonplace, not only in Chicago but also in New York and London, although its application in England was frequently associated with residential uses. Yet, apart from associations with its precedents, this window type was specific to Loos's building insofar as it was sized, proportioned, and detailed to accommodate practical situations on either side of the facade, particularly on the inside. The Looshaus was built as a specialized department store for the firm of Goldman and Salatsch, whose advertisements appeared in Loos's publication *Das Andere*. While the entry level of the building is given over to the display and sale of a range of merchandise, the mezzanine level, behind the bay windows, houses a number of settings for the storage, cutting and sewing, display, and sale of cloth and men's suits. In most of these situations abundant light is necessary. In others, such as the fitting rooms, privacy is required as well. In still other places, light is required, along with a view, whereas in other areas ventilation is needed. The use of different glazing types allowed Loos to acknowledge these several requirements and to modulate ambient conditions. But the consistent use of one type of glazing also allowed him to give the entire level compositional uniformity. Within the thickness of the facade he had the depth of the bay window to work with, and thus was able to variously dispose display tables, seating, work surfaces, and storage shelves. The great quantity of glazing also favored the illumination of the edges of the central volume, which otherwise would have been too dark because of the building's considerable plan depth. The use of mirrors and the *Raumplan* section also helped increase light levels in the depth of the interior. When seen from the outside, these facade openings are expressive not only of modern precedents but of specific patterns of commercial practice, endowing their representational function with performative substance. The same can be said for the openings above and below the mezzanine level, making the facade as a whole a set of figures determined as much by functionality as association.

WINDOWS AND/AS WALLS

When Pierre Chareau accounted for the history of the window wall facade of the Maison de Verre (1931), he explained: "[When] I had to build between two party walls . . . there was only one way to get the maximum amount of light. . . . The principle of doing away with windows was adopted. . . . [When the] elements that [were to be] assembled [were chosen] . . . the Nevada type of glass lens seemed to correspond best to the conditions of the problem."[41] With the comprehensive use of glass brick, light was indeed maximized, but so too was privacy, which was not only desired but necessary. As is well known, the house was

DAS ANDERE

EIN BLATT ZUR EINFUEHRUNG ABENDLAENDISCHER KULTUR IN OESTERREICH: GESCHRIEBEN VON ADOLF LOOS   I. JAHR

TAILORS AND OUTFITTERS

GOLDMAN & SALATSCH

K. U. K. HOF-
LIEFERANTEN
K. BAYER. HOF-
LIEFERANTEN

KAMMER-
LIEFERANTEN
Sr. k. u. k. Hoheit des
Herrn Erzherzog Josef
etc. etc.

WIEN, I. GRABEN 20.

HALM & GOLDMANN

ANTIQUARIATS-BUCHHANDLUNG
für Wissenschaft, Kunst und Literatur

WIEN, I. BABENBERGERSTRASSE 5

Großes Lager von wertvollen Werken aus allen
Wissenschaften.

Einrichtung von belletristischen und Volksbiblio-
theken.

Ankauf von ganzen Bibliotheken und einzelnen
Werken aus allen Zweigen des Wissens.

Übernahme von Bücher- und Autographen-
auktionen unter kulantesten Bedingungen.

COXIN das neue Mittel zur Entwicklung
photographischer Platten, Rollfilms

ohne **DUNKELKAMMER**

bei Tages- oder künstlichem Licht ist in allen
einschlägigen Geschäften zu haben.

COXIN ist kein gefärbter Entwickler. — COXIN
erfordert keinerlei neue Apparate und kann immer
benutzt werden.

COXIN-EXPORTGESELLSCHAFT
Wien, VII/2, Breitegasse 3.

3.14
Cover of *Das Andere* with advertise-
ment for Goldman & Salatsch, 1903.

3.15
Adolf Loos,
Goldman & Salatsch store (Looshaus),
detail, Vienna, 1911.

3.16
Pierre Chareau, Maison de Verre,
exterior, Paris, 1931.
Photo: Charles H. Tashima, 1991.

3.17
Pierre Chareau, Maison de Verre,
interior, Paris, 1931.

built to enclose not only domestic settings on the upper two floors but Dr. D'Alsace's medical practice on the ground level, which required not only bright and uniform light but privacy. The glass brick, previously unused in such an application, met both needs. Upstairs, as an enclosing element for the house's main living spaces, the glass also suited the family's needs. Yet, while it was used comprehensively, glass brick was not used everywhere on the exterior walls, for other settings required connections to the exterior that the glass brick could not afford. An example is the doctor's ground-floor study, which is the only setting that gives onto the rear garden. The room required uniform lighting, as did other settings in the house, and the glass brick worked fine for that purpose; but it also benefited from apertures that permitted views into the garden and the introduction of fresh air into the space. Windows in the top half of the doors serve the second of these purposes, the doors themselves the first. Through much of the house, ventilation is mechanical, but in some spaces—along the second-floor hallway, for example—windows that rotate on a pivot can be opened one at a time or all together. Like the rest of the "equipment" in the house, they are operable or performative. A number of critics have described these devices as both functional and poetic, indicating with this second term an aesthetic or figurative content that resulted from imaginative attention to thematics of light and hygiene. The "workings" of the building and its facades show how windows and window walls can serve both constructional and representational purposes—as long as the subject matter of the representation includes the typical practices that occur behind the facade, with the facade as one of their furnishings.

This accent on the operations of the window or wall was not Chareau's alone; it had been seen in modern buildings before his, in those of Loos, Perret, and Le Corbusier. It can be seen in projects of later decades too. Perhaps the best summary to this argument is a text published in 1962 entitled "Windows and Walls," in which José Luis Sert observed that "for thousands of years, from the doors of the caves until recently, all windows . . . served the triple function of providing light, ventilation and view."[42] Here Sert restated the topics of concern that were apparent in the Maison de Verre and the Looshaus, as well as other examples: apertures illuminate interiors, allow those settings to breathe, and frame exterior landscapes. Sert developed his theme by writing a brief history of aperture types (as if he accepted Le Corbusier's assertion that the history of architecture is nothing more than the story of how architects have opened windows in walls). Like Le Corbusier, Sert described the epochal change that resulted from

3.18
Sert, Jackson and Gourley, married
student housing, Harvard University,
Cambridge, 1965.

the substitution of masonry construction with steel frame structures, for this building technique transformed walls—both inside and out—into screens: "with the introduction of steel and concrete skeletons . . . the nature of walls [was transformed] from bearing walls to nonbearing partitions, curtain or screen walls."[43] This change did not lead to the neglect of the three functions outlined above, but to their reconsideration as the basic components of facade design. An important step forward in the redefinition of the wall of windows was the invention and use of the sun-breaker or *brise-soleil.* But not all architects operating in the postwar years followed Le Corbusier's lead; others took a step backward by encasing their office buildings with uninterrupted plates of glass: "modules that repeat [themselves] from bottom to skyline." These are the facades of "anonymity" that came to be criticized with such vehemence a decade and a half later. The alternative for Sert involved reconsideration of scale as a way of preserving (or reinventing) the link between people and buildings. His alternative also involved attention to both the range of materials available to the architect and the range of "performances" the wall was meant to achieve. Sert's approach to the problem of civic representation and monumentality led him to recommend the collaboration of artists, sculptors, and architects in the development of facades that would restore figurative substance to city centers. In this paper, too, he turned to aesthetic problems, concluding that "the growth and rebuilding of cities demands a more complete and varied vocabulary." The "play" of elements, whether transparent, translucent, or opaque, was important to Sert, whether they were deployed in a wall with windows or a wall of windows. He preferred neither operable nor sealed elements, but recommended both. Just as significant as the play of elements was that of dwelling practices—the cultural play that prompted the selection and configuration of specific elements, practices such as viewing, breathing, lighting, shading, or sheltering—because the performance of a window wall has as its most basic task the orchestration of human events, those it encloses and reveals.

The progressive substitution of thin, lightweight, and transparent elements of enclosure for thick, heavy, and opaque walls would seem to have completed itself in our time, were it not for the fact that many of the opportunities for figuration in architecture—especially those associated with thick-wall construction—remain unexplored within the context of modern building. The victory of thin over thick would be a hollow one indeed if it marked the end of the building's role in mediating private and public life, or interiors and their surroundings, for this is one way, perhaps the most important way, in which architecture gives durable dimension to the patterns of our culture.

It would be naive, however, to assume that the industrialized products that have been at hand in the twentieth century have performed this role simply because they are "modern" or were manufactured in modern times. The fact that much of twentieth-century building has contributed to the disintegration of our cities and landscapes into a spread of anonymous or autobiographical set pieces suggests alternative explanations of the modern inheritance. One of these, popular since the emergence of postmodernism in architecture, regards the negative consequences of modern building practices as sufficient grounds for proposing a return to thick-wall construction, whether in fact or in appearance. This would be accomplished by a return to preindustrial methods of construction or by the development of the clearest possible distinction between the inner, insignificant and industrialized parts of a building and its outer, figurative and "designed" parts. The tide of this reactionary view, and the practices it sustains, have variously ebbed and flowed throughout the past few decades, as has confidence in industrialized building itself. Surprising as it may seem, these arguments for and against industrialized building, and in particular the arguments for and against the thin or insubstantial wall, have much in common. They both proceed from the assumption that architectural form is determined by a system, whether of building or of signifying. From our point of view, to require a choice between a lightweight and a heavy architecture, or between an abstract and a figurative one, is both misleading and unacceptable. Instead, we choose to describe how architecture can perform its cultural role while being variously thick and thin, transparent and opaque, and to envisage an architecture that acknowledges this performance as one of its roles.

In twentieth-century architecture, the substitution of lightweight for heavy elements has sustained the development of new ways in which architecture can perform its mediating role. Just as transparency does not always contribute to cultural sense, so embodiment of meaning does not depend upon thickness or depth. While the dematerialization of the wall can result in vacuous and impoverished architecture, it can also allow for the development of new modes of figuration. The first stage of this development was the formulation of a conceptual distinction between the outer and inner elements of the wall, designating the former— the shell, skin, cladding, or covering—as the non-load-bearing or atectonic part.

ATECTONIC FABRICATIONS: SLIDING SURFACES

The fabric analogy for architectural cladding had wide currency in Austrian and German architecture in the early years of the twentieth century. While Otto Wagner, Josef Hoffmann, and Max Fabiani drew on the teachings of Gottfried Semper for this analogy, each interpreted it differently. The complexity of the topic is revealed in these differences.[1] In Hoffmann's Palais Stoclet (1911), for example, the application of moldings around the edges of the stone cladding reinforces the planar quality of the material. The facade, made of brick and faced with sheets of white Turili marble, resists a three-dimensional reading as a tectonic mass. Eduard Sekler has described these non-load-bearing marble surfaces as atectonic.[2] The interior of the house is also clad with thin sheets of materials that conceal structural elements such as columns, beams, piers, or arches, resulting in surface planarity. On the exterior, the impression of thinness is strengthened by the placement of windows flush with the outer surface. Nevertheless, the crucial moment occurs when the surface planes must be joined, or turned around a corner. At such junctures, a tubular motif made of gilded black metal is used to

4.1
Herzog and de Meuron, signal box, Auf dem Wolf,
Basel, 1995.

4.2

Josef Hoffmann, Palais Stoclet, facade,
Brussels, 1911.

conceal the connection, giving the facade the appearance of upholstery articulated with sewn piping.[3]

In upholstery and in dressmaking, piping—a cord enclosed in a pipelike fold—serves as the trimming or ornamentation of edges or seams. A similar joining technique may be found in confectionery, where the cordlike lines are made of sugar. In neither case is the support of a surface, or "load bearing," indicated; such bands run both horizontally and vertically, indifferent to gravity and displaying no trace of "tectonic expression." Precedents for this detail exist in traditional construction, a famous example being Ca d'Oro in Venice, where the rope molding is stone. In Hoffmann's architecture, piping serves the purpose of mediating the size of the individual stone panels with the bulk of the whole building, establishing a set of intermediate planes that could be read as virtually independent of one another. Because the width of the panel joints is negligible and each panel is the same size (from the bottom to the top of the facade and from side to side), each section retains an apparent independence both from the other sections and from the mass of the building. The flattened effect of this is similar to that of the paintings on the interior of the Palais Stoclet, which were made by Hoffmann's friend and collaborator, Gustav Klimt.

Inside the building the pilasters are flattened or suppressed, again like the bodies depicted by Klimt: in both cases, volume or thickness is subordinated to surface, allowing the sliding and gliding of elements past one another in the shallow depth of the surface. Thinning the plane and its elements in this way, and compressing the depth into a shallow surface, tends to free the cladding from the building in a manner reminiscent of the free planarity of the De Stijl architecture of Gerrit Rietveld and J. J. P. Oud.[4] Thus, in moving from inside to outside, there are two types of "free cladding": one that is enriched (and, together with Klimt's images, "oneiric"), and one that is impoverished or abstract. In neither case is the cladding "constructive."

On Max Fabiani's Portois and Fix block of flats in Vienna (1899–1900),[5] the cladding is also "freed," but with important differences: the middle three stories can be read as a tableau or plane that is punctured by a series of regularly shaped vertical windows. In its planarity this wall resembles the Palais Stoclet, yet it has rhythm and depth. The surface is composed of tiles in incremental shades of green and brown, which are arranged in a rectangular pattern and bonded to the load-bearing wall behind. The tension between the regularity of this pattern

4.3
Max Fabiani,
Portois and Fix apartments,
Vienna, 1900.

and the gradations of color intensity generates a rhythm of changing effects that results in the dematerialization of the building's surface. The reflection of light off the tiles creates a surface luminosity that brightens the street—a quality for which the building was praised at the time.[6] While this shining tableau of three stories has a typically urban composition of base, middle, and top, the surface pattern constitutes a free facade, inasmuch as the main vertical bays and elements of the base and top are interrupted by the atectonic surface of the intermediate horizontal band. Here, too, a comparison with Klimt's paintings might be apt because in both cases we see the same horizontal spread or drift of figures from side to side. The Portois and Fix facade can also be compared to Hoffmann's interiors, or to the decorated tiled surfaces of Oriental architecture as well as more recent facades by Venturi, Rauch and Scott Brown.

Yet the facade of the Portois and Fix flats is not only patterned but also colored, and in this respect it bears a resemblance to pointillism.[7] In pointillist paintings, a whole range of different hues and tonal values are balanced with each other. When such a treatment is applied to the surface of a building, the colors used need not indicate constructional materials; they can instead exemplify an "art of pure color," which in our time might illustrate a "philosophy of paint."[8] On the Portois and Fix building, as we have noted, Fabiani combined tiles of different shades and tints of pale green and brown. Despite the restricted palette, the tonal color values are mixed (again) by the viewer's eye. This effect was well known to pointillist painters, who employed complementary colors that merged with one another and with ambient light to create an additive or synthetic tonal value. The same qualities were also thought of by Louis Sullivan, but he used the analogy of an Oriental carpet (he speaks of the similarity between the cladding of a building and the appearance of an "Anatolian rug"). Thus the visual qualities of the surface of the Portois and Fix facade were developed independently of the wall's tectonic conditions: the cladding is thin, superficial, and pictorial. Unlike Hoffmann's cladding, however, it is radiant.

In addition to considerations of pattern and surface, ideas about perceptual vantage points contributed to the design of this and other contemporary Viennese facades. For Otto Wagner, a building in a narrow street required flatter ornament, or a "more delicate structure," than one located on a wide avenue.[9] Modern architecture, in his account, would emerge from optical principles—from calculations of specific viewing points, of the eye's need for repose, and of the best opportunities for concentrated viewing. This flattening was a form of

4.4

Georges Seurat, *Sunday Afternoon on the Island of La Grande Jatte,* detail, 1886.

"realism" for Wagner, both of pictorial vision and of city building, and would lead to the convergence of tectonic, sculptural, and urban form.

MASKING AND REVEALING

Wagner's early work, however, reveals not an atectonic but a pictorial treatment of the architectural surface.[10] This is evident in the Majolica House (1889), for example, where the pattern of the cladding, though not geometric, adds a decorative surface to a load-bearing construction. The textilelike pattern is organic and floral.[11] In Wagner's later work, such as the Karlsplatz station (1896–1898), his treatment of the surface changes: the cladding imagery includes both organic and constructional figures that follow the traditional tripartite composition of urban buildings. Here, the figurative elements on the upper part of the building's facades consist of flora; the uppermost border, for example, is ringed by sunflowers. On the middle and lower parts, however, the panels, metal pilasters, and joints have been sized, shaped, and polished in accordance with the logic of construction.[12] The intervals between the pilasters and their width are determined by the bays of the load-bearing frame, yet the pilasters themselves are not load-bearing, nor is the rusticated stone of the base. The image presented by this building does not disavow construction—as did other contemporary Viennese projects by Wagner himself or by others—nor does it simply reveal the building's load-bearing structure and materials, according to the tenets of "structural rationalism"; revealed instead are new modes of construction (and structural forms) through a novel treatment of old materials. The stone of the base is not supporting but supported, not solid walling but infill panels. Its appearance recalls the logic of traditional methods of construction: *Artis sola domina necessitas* (Necessity is the mother of invention).

"The architect must always develop the form of art from construction," wrote Wagner in *Moderne Architektur,* in which he idealizes *Baukunst* (the art of building).[13] His approach to cladding could embody in ironic form the tensions between an architecture that acknowledges modern realities and one that defers to traditional forms. In Wagner's Post Office Savings Bank (1904–1906), the stone base is of a classical character, but at the corners a "modern" thinness is revealed, thus exposing the artificiality of this gesture. This practice constitutes both a masking and a revealing, a form of construction that distinguishes itself

4.5

Otto Wagner, Majolica House,
Vienna, 1889.

4.6
Otto Wagner,
church of St. Leopold am Steinhof,
Vienna, 1907. Photo: Charles H.
Tashima, 1991.

4.7
Otto Wagner, Post Office Savings
Bank, Vienna, 1906. Photo: Charles H.
Tashima, 1991.

from itself, resulting in an idealized or denaturalized art of building. The discrepancies and disjunctions between the frontal (heavy) and the side (light) views are reinscribed onto the facade, allowing the viewer to perceive the mutually opposed aspects of its self-presentation. Nevertheless, so important had building (*Baukunst*) become in Wagner's thinking that he revised the title of *Moderne Architektur* to *Die Baukunst unserer Zeit* in its last edition (1914).

SYMBOLIC SURFACES

Wagner, Hoffmann, and Fabiani were obviously indebted to Gottfried Semper's idea of the "dematerialized" character of the architectural surface,[14] for it is this interpretation of architectural symbols which opened up the possibility of developing the atectonic facade. Semper argued that "the haze of carnival candles is the true atmosphere of art. This annihilation of reality, of the material, is necessary if form is to emerge as a meaningful symbol, as an autonomous creation of man."[15] This "annihilation" of reality and of material is most apparent when the architectural covering is a product of the application of "pure color," a subject that had interested Semper from the earliest part of his career, when he published his first paper on polychromy. In his later writings, and specifically in the section of *Der Stil* devoted to Hellenistic art, Semper described color as the most subtle and bodiless of covering materials, capable of "masking" the materiality of stone so that it appears as pure form.[16] Thus, he argued, architectural expression was not limited solely to the representation of construction (as advocated by theorists such as Carlo Lodoli, Karl Bötticher, and Eugène-Emmanuel Viollet-le-Duc). Surface forms and applied colors symbolized human events. Like mimesis in the theater, which entails the masking of the actor's feelings to make way for the characterization of his role, architectural mimesis masks the materials so that symbolic content can emerge. Semper believed that monumental architecture had originated in commemorative drama, "where the masking or denial of reality is fundamental to the religious or secular event."[17] A textile pattern on an architectural surface thus has as its mimetic referent the interweaving of people in dance and other communal activities, as much as the weaving of reeds and grasses. Wall building is therefore symbolic of the building of community. The urban role that both Fabiani and Wagner envisaged for their buildings echoes this sense of cladding or dressing as inseparable from community or culture. For Semper, the "pure" colors and forms of cladding reinforced the fabric of a community while also

4.8
Otto Wagner, Schützenhaus, Vienna,
1907. Photo: Charles H. Tashima,
1991.

recalling its origins in festival apparatus.[18] This included temporary fixtures such as drapes, carpets, boughs, festoons, garlands, trophies, and flowers, the "equipment" of commemoration (*die Festapparatus*) or improvised scaffolding.[19] These were used in the presentation of special events, which themselves were symbolic embodiments of the extremes of everyday life (the greatest pain and suffering or the most complete satisfaction, argued Aristotle). In tragic drama, mimesis does not "represent" what is already there but indicates what could or ought to be, hence its fictive nature. Monumental architecture, too, is fictive, for it assumes the denial of reality. Cladding or dressing, for Semper, invites the spectator to participate in an atectonic "as if"; that is, the building appears as if it were built in other materials in another time. Although the building materials are not themselves represented, they must nevertheless be understood and mastered in the process of construction; this is a necessary condition of their denial. No masking is possible if what lies behind the mask is false. In this way the atemporal reinscribes the temporal, recalling for coming generations the origin of monuments in festive occasions. Accordingly, architecture originated in dressing, as Loos was later to assert in his "Principles of Cladding."

Many German idealists had put forward similar arguments. Schlegel, Schelling, and Goethe each in different ways advanced the argument that architecture's claim to the status of fine art precluded an exclusive emphasis on the functional and utilitarian aspects of building. Schlegel asserted that architecture must imitate itself as an art of need, and further that it "must portray the inorganic as the allegory of the organic . . . to portray the former as the essence of the latter . . . within the inorganic, that is, such that the latter is not itself organic but rather merely signifies or means the organic. Yet, precisely this is the nature of allegory."[20] For Schlegel, art transcended its material nature by imitating the processes and relationships of nature. Semper and Karl Bötticher developed their ideas about core forms and art forms within the context of this tradition.[21]

In England, too, there were advocates of the use of "immaterial" form and pure color in architectural cladding. One of the most widely disseminated treatises on the subject was Owen Jones's *The Grammar of Ornament* (1856), in which he relates man's natural creativity to surface decoration: "To this feeling must be ascribed the tattooing of the human face and body, resorted to by the savage. . . . As we advance higher, from the decoration of the rude tent or wigwam to the sublime works of a Phidias and Praxiteles, the same feeling is everywhere

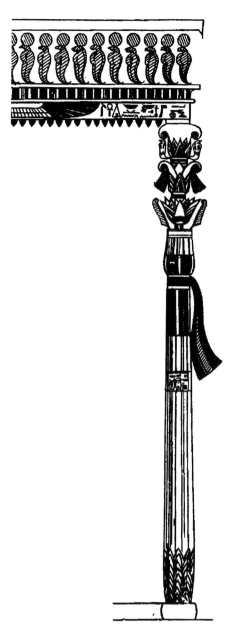

4.9

Gottfried Semper, *Festapparatus,*
from *Der Stil in den technischen und
tektonischen Künsten* (1860–1863).

apparent: the highest ambition is still to create, to stamp on this earth the impress of an individual mind."[22]

THE IMPRESSED FACADE: TATTOO

In the case of a tattoo, such an "impress" is immaterial; the tattoo supplements the surface of the body as it covers it. Jones includes in his treatise an illustration of a tattooed face on which there are marks that elaborate the profile. Semper had argued that the marks tattooed on people of certain cultures often conformed to the shape of the body, especially that of the underlying bone structure and musculature.[23] Likewise, colored tattoos highlighted skin color—black on surfaces in shadow, red on the lips. However, this claim was contradicted by Alois Riegl, who observed in *Problems of Style* that tattoos on the faces of the Maori were spiral in shape, obviously not following the lines or folds of the body.[24] This observation replaces Jones's idea of the tattoo as an "impress" with a more abstract conception. For Riegl the geometric stylization of natural forms in the arts preceded their role as symbols. Accordingly, while symbols may have originated as fetishes exhibiting a visual continuity with the appearance of something that occurs in nature, they often lost their direct connection to nature through geometric stylization. This, he believed, explained the difficulty of distinguishing ornament from symbol.[25]

In 1769, when Captain Cook first introduced Europeans to the people of Tahiti and their practices, he described how "both sexes paint their bodies, tattow, as it is called in their language. This is done by inlaying the color of black under their skins, in such a manner as to be indelible."[26] It was, he recorded, so painful a process that very few had their faces tattooed—more often it was the buttocks—but, wherever the marks were made, they were applied only once in a lifetime. Permanence was thus considered an essential characteristic of the tattoo. The tattoo is a form of "self"-defining adornment which, unlike jewelry, cannot be exchanged or passed on to another person.[27] It is also a type of figure—a set of lines, shapes, and colors—that both denies the deeper "reality" (or autonomous and unsocialized character) of the bearer and elicits attention and admiration. This is its social function, which is analogous to the function of such a mark on a building in an urban context.

Is tattoo art thus an instance of "disfiguration," inspiring repugnance in "us," or is it figuration, representing signs of self-definition? Can we distinguish

4.10

New Zealand face, from Owen Jones,
The Grammar of Ornament (1856).

it from other types of cosmetic art, some form of which everyone practices every day? "For most African peoples, a child is by definition not yet civilized, by which is meant enculturated and socialized [without these signs] . . . a Maori without moko (tattoo) is not a complete person. More broadly, changes in role and status are often reflected in distinctive regimes of body art; in their irreversible forms, the traces of such alterations of the body amount to a kind of biographical accumulation—a dynamic, cumulative instrumentality representing the palimpsest of intense experiences which define the evolving person."[28]

This sort of anthropological view was not of course available in the nineteenth century, and Loos could only conceive of the tattoo as a superficial excrescence—for him it was associated with the criminal class as much as with primitive cultures. He condemned inscribed or applied ornament as degenerate, or at best mere decoration, and advocated its elimination. As mentioned earlier, Riegl had observed that distinguishing ornamental from symbolic geometry was difficult. Presumably Loos believed that the "ornamental" columns at the entry to his Looshaus were not stylized, that is, mere ornament, nor would he see the "iconic" column of his design for the Chicago Tribune building as merely ornamental.

Loos's argument rejecting tattooed markings could be extended to reject all cosmetic ornaments. On this point his views clearly differed from those of Semper, who suggested that color applied to the body heightens or elaborates natural hue: red on red lips, for example. The same could be said of geometry: vertical lines make what is tall appear taller. Loos's "law of cladding" rejects both forms of ornamentation. For him, the proper ornamentation of a surface results not from the application of color or lines, but from the cultivation or nurturing of the qualities that are natural and proper to a given subject. If Vienna is a "limewash city," as he claimed, this is a consequence of local geology and craft traditions, both cultivated for centuries. In this respect, the white surfaces of the upper floors of the Michaelerhaus can be regarded as ornamental and typical. In an argument reminiscent of Plato's idea that beauty in a person results from diet and health rather than paint and dressing,[29] Loos claimed that women's preference for ornamental and colorful effects (long skirts covering their legs, for example) explains the retarded development of their fashions.[30] He contrasted women's fashion with men's, in which colorful "effects" are not decisive and shape and pattern result from the needs of posture and movement. For men, contemporary conditions of work necessitated the performance of tasks that could not be accomplished in traditional "ornamental" costume. Loos's thesis identifies propriety not as a moral code but as a standard of performance, and it shifts the emphasis from appearance to action, or what people typically do. Thus surfaces can be treated as figures, images, and ornament, but these must emerge from concrete practice.

Would Loos, had he been writing in our time rather than that of Freud's Vienna, still have argued that marks reflect criminal tendencies? His interpretation of tattoos provided him with a metaphor by means of which the progress of civilization could be measured: "The Papuan and the criminal ornament their skin, the Indian covers his paddle and his boat with layers and layers of ornament. But the bicycle and the steam engine are free of ornament. The march of civilization systematically liberates object after object from ornamentation."[31] It therefore seems likely that Loos would have been critical of Fabiani's Portois and Fix building, but also of his Casa Bartoli and Das Haus "Zum Roten Igel," with their tattoolike facades. Yet, if surface marks like the tattoo have the social and urban function of conferring a recognizable identity on their bearer, must we not ask whether their elimination would lead to the weakening of such a structure—whether a social group or a city?

Loos had other arguments against ornament. Women's dress was incompatible with the freedom to work beside, or even to compete with, men. Thus the absence of ornament was a sign of liberation in economic life as well as in relations of gender. This social and indeed economic reasoning coexisted with Loos's revulsion at the savage's willingness to defile the body.

SURFACE APPLIQUÉ

Arguing for an ornamented surface, Robert Venturi has also invoked the savage or "primitive" sensibility, but unlike Loos he advocates "learning from" what he described in 1982 as the "primitive vernacular."[32] The surface patterns in "primitive" art constitute, in his account, the "essence of style," and as such can be found in all sorts of architecture, whether heroic or folk—in the early work of Gunnar Asplund, for example, as well as in the American or Alpine domestic vernacular. Ornament, for Venturi, has a symbolic function, as it did for Semper, though in a different sense; and like Semper's *isthmia* wreath, ornament is meant to communicate a sense of community. But the comparison with Semper has its limits, for Venturi's definition of surface appliqué as "independent of the architecture in content and form" and having "nothing to do with the spatial or structural elements" to which they are applied more closely resembles Riegl's stance that ornament may or may not be symbolic.[33] Likewise, Venturi's use of facade ornament is closer to Fabiani's Portois and Fix flats than it is to Wagner's Post Office Savings Bank. Thus conceived, pattern as representation "involves the depiction as opposed to the construction of symbol and ornament"; it is "freer and less consistent," "abstract" but "pretty"—like Muslim, Byzantine, or Victorian stylized motifs.

This series of definitions of appliqué restates the position adopted earlier by Venturi, Scott Brown, and Izenour in their definition of the "decorated shed": "systems of space and structure are directly at the service of program [in the shed], and ornament is applied independently of them. This we call the decorated shed."[34] Their design for the Institute for Scientific Information in Philadelphia (1979) clearly exemplifies this definition. The "shed" for the ISI was determined by the client's requirement for a building that could be expanded in the future. The result was a "modernist" box with strip windows and a lateral placement of circulation and core elements. But the client also wanted a building "that everyone would recognize as a lively and distinctive contribution to the community and to the information industry,"[35] and it is this requirement that led to the design of a "decorated" facade.

The building's exterior is made of uniformly colored brickwork, with no distinction between top and bottom or from side to side. Into the wall that serves as the front elevation have been inserted continuous horizontal windows in six sections. A single section of these wraps around the side wall flanking the entryway. The other openings on this side wall are grouped into local symmetries. All of this—the brickwork as well as the windows—acts as a canvas to which has been added a colored geometrical pattern: "Our design distinguishes the building from its surroundings by imposing on the facade a geometrical pattern of colored brick and porcelain panels. The tight, rigorously coded pattern of the overall facade is relieved by the juxtaposition of large abstracted flower forms marking the main entrance to the building."[36] These porcelain panels have a symmetrical layout, white and uniform at the center, bleeding out toward the right and left, and this symmetry is reinforced by the lettering on the facade. The horizontal emphasis of the facade is countered by brightly colored vertical panels in the gaps between the central windows, giving the impression of engaged or interwoven pilasters. The contradictions between the facade's centrality and its seriality, as

4.11
Venturi, Rauch and Scott Brown,
Institute for Scientific Information,
Philadelphia, 1979.

well as between its horizontal and vertical elements, were intended to create a sense of ambiguity, or "both/and"; in this case, they also gave rise to the building's "lively" and "distinctive" presence. Like the tattoo described by Owen Jones, the building's pattern is an "impress," a stamp or imprint that signifies through a geometry which is derived less from the "body" it covers than from the graphic interests and pictorial imagination of its maker.

Venturi's intentions were that this impress or impression should be visible from the street, both to people driving past the building and to pedestrians. Yet the two modes of transportation imply different vantage points. Acknowledgment of the street is apparent in the positioning of the entry, which recedes as an angle perpendicular to approaching traffic. The upper level—the spread pattern—invites views from cars traveling in both directions. The dispersed dots at the edges anticipate centrality and symmetry. However, this effect is only apparent from a stationary point in front of the building and gives the impression of a changing surface, a "lively" facade that recalls Wagner's ideas about vantage points in an urban context. Yet, unlike the Portois and Fix building, where windows puncture the planar, tiled surface, the decorated surfaces of the ISI building are interrupted by the continuous strip windows. As a result, this facade lacks continuity—of both surface and pattern. Frontality is established but also destabilized; no view or viewpoint is privileged, or at least the view from the automobile is just as important as the pedestrian's view. Moreover, the openness of the site, together with the presence of nearby buildings of different heights, prevents viewers from focusing on the surface features of the building. Rather, it is the volume that registers at first and last glance.

The setting of the ISI is very different from the tight urban fabric surrounding the Portois and Fix building, which allows only a glancing impression of the facade. The subtle and unsettling tonal variations of Fabiani's green facade have been replaced on the ISI building by a polychrome pattern that is more didactic and cheerful. The facade clearly distinguishes itself from its surroundings, but we may wonder whether this building is an illustration of Riegl's anxiety about the difficulty of distinguishing between ornament and symbol.

IMPRESSIONS

At the turn of the century, other architects than Wagner were concerned with the way that buildings could be experienced in the modern city. While this concern also figured prominently in Camillo Sitte's account of the experiential aspects of the modern city as an important element of urban design,[37] it received a more extensive treatment in H. P. Berlage's papers on architecture and impressionism.[38] Berlage's argument for a "radical reform" of architecture, presented under the heading of "impressionism," encompassed the modern city as well as the traditional town, the latter the focus of Sitte's arguments. In concentrating on surface impressions, Berlage subordinated the architectural detail to the appearance of the whole, and the whole to the overall impression, giving the subjective view priority over objective analysis. The building surface, or "pattern," was meant to inscribe into its geometry the varying viewpoints of urban experience.

An excellent example of this approach to cladding design is Berlage's Holland House in London (1914). The street frontage of the site is so narrow that only an oblique view of the building is possible. The facade is composed of glazed columns rising from pavement to roof, spaced a little over a meter apart and corresponding to the bays of the load-bearing frame behind. When viewing the facade, the short distance between each of the columns, together with the depth of each recessed bay, virtually eliminates any sense of the windowed surfaces behind. Thus the facade appears as an unbroken plane. This plane is not flat, however, nor is it uniform, for the gray-green glazed terra-cotta tiles covering the columns cause it to reflect light throughout the day, creating a vibrant effect. From the 1880s onward, Berlage had been using glazed tiles inside his buildings, invariably white or yellow tiles in stairwells and lightwells. In the last decade of the century he used them with greater frequency on exteriors, a practice for which there was ample precedent in Dutch buildings from the sixteenth century onward, when the manufacture of tiles became widespread.

But it was in 1892 that Berlage first conceived of an "impressionistic architecture that would appeal to the viewer through mass, relief, silhouette and extremely economically applied sculpture alone."[39] The facade of Holland House could be said to resemble a canvas by an impressionist painter such as Monet, in that it is expansive, shallow in depth, and subtly varying in its chromatic radiance—in short, uniform but also unstable. In the paintings of Monet, Seurat, and Signac, there is an obvious concentration on light, to such a degree that the image becomes identified with its play. Light is not represented but revealed. Everything about the painting and its handling, which seemed so unfinished, so rough, even primitive to many at the time, serves this purpose. The subject matter—sky, water, fields, etc.—is removed from conventional settings in order to

4.12
H. P. Berlage, Holland House,
London, 1914. Photo © V. Bennett
1996.

strengthen the concentration on light; in a sense, the subject matter is also painting itself. Colors, light, and surfaces in the "finished" work are mixed not on the painter's palette nor on the canvas but in the productive gaze of the spectator, resulting in a cooperative synthesis of the image, a *mélange optique* that depends on the observer's participation.[40] This mixing results in an intensification of surface radiation. The chemist Michel Chevreul in his book *The Law of Simultaneous Contrast,* first published in 1839, had put forward the hypothesis that complementary colors, when juxtaposed on a surface and joined together by the eye, mutually intensified one another. Observations of this phenomenon led to the development of the "law of simultaneous contrast."

Unlike an impressionist canvas, however, the facade of Holland House reinforces horizons of brightness beyond its own limits: the columns become incrementally thinner as they rise, making the wall appear darker at the base yet virtually transparent at the top. This grading of light levels exemplifies the way Berlage used facade impressions to shape a site and a street.

The same could be said of the Sanderson and Company factory, built by C. F. A. Voysey in Chiswick at about the same time (1902). The white glazed bricks used on the facade of this building illuminate the narrow street on its entry side, as well as the older factory building next to it. On the subject of a building's radiance, Voysey wrote: "The essential idea suggested by light is activity, and the chief material consequence is cleanliness. We all like abundance of light for work and play. It stimulates action."[41] For both Voysey and Berlage, architectural cladding presented an opportunity for the building to transcend its physical limits through the use of light in combination with modern means of construction, thereby sustaining both work and play. In both cases, the architects conceived of modern construction practices and figurative motifs in relation to particular conditions and aspirations of social life rather than as possessing their own autonomous logic.

PLANARITY AND SURFACE IMPRESSIONS

How do architectural surfaces such as these differ from those of any postwar International Style building? Or how does this kind of geometry differ from that of more recent steel frame buildings, such as Mies van der Rohe's Lake Shore Drive apartment buildings? Mies, too, was interested in visual effects and in the optical impressions created by surface pattern. In his first publication, which

4.13
C. F. A. Voysey,
Sanderson and Company
factory, London, 1902.

described his design for a glass skyscraper in 1922, he explained that he had "angled the respective facade fronts . . . to avoid the danger of an effect of lifelessness . . . [and] achieve a rich interplay of light reflections."[42] This facade, like that of the ISI, was meant to be "lively." To explain Mies's preoccupation with geometrical form, Fritz Neumeyer has claimed that he was primarily interested in the outward appearance of his buildings, that is, in aesthetic rather than technological concerns.[43] On this point, at least, Venturi, Scott Brown, and Izenour agree with Mies. In *Learning from Las Vegas,* they tried to clarify their own intentions with reference to what they took to be his: "Less may have been more . . . but the 'I' section on Mies van der Rohe's columns, for instance, is as complexly ornamental as the applied pilaster on the Renaissance pier, or the incised shaft in the Gothic pier. (In fact, less was more work.)"[44] They went on to argue that "Mies' 'I' section appliqués represent naked steel frame construction," for their purpose is to signify at the same time as they conceal the frame beneath.[45]

In *Learning from Las Vegas,* Mies is criticized for limiting the "symbolism," or structural ornament, of a building to its strictly architectural elements—"the honest expression of modern technology as space," as he himself described it. Yet, in fact, signification for him had content that embraced much more than architecture. The skeletal frame possesses an aura of "somber primitivity," he wrote. "Primitive," or raw, in this usage intends surfaces that are undressed or unclad; it is perhaps best exemplified in the well-known portrait of Mies standing before the structural frame of the Farnsworth House. Mies was not alone in his admiration for the simple or the primitive in frame construction; his contemporary Karl Scheffler, a great apologist for Gothic architecture, spoke of the strong sensations one experiences in front of a half-finished project.[46] Clearly Venturi, Scott Brown, and Izenour overestimate the purely architectural content of the type of signification Mies intended; it was not so much the symbolization of architecture that he valued, as the expression of the primitive, synonymous for him with the irreducible, beautiful, and true—the "naked truth." (For many years, Mies kept open on his drafting table a copy of Leo Frobenius's *Das unbekannte Afrika,* an anthropological and ethnographic study containing images of architecture and artifacts as well as people, some wearing tattoos.)[47]

Nakedness for Mies, whether of buildings or of bodies, does not claim authenticity but acknowledges its own representational character. William Jordy's term for the skeletal frame, "laconic splendor,"[48] is useful in this connection because it combines a sense of the restraint and the excess that coexist in the buildings of Mies. If the structural frame was self-effacing, it was also sublime, that is, both tacit and overwhelming—reduced to fullness—and this quality was most apparent when a construction was still in progress, when the "pattern" of beams and columns stood out by itself. Mies wrote in 1922 that "only skyscrapers under construction reveal the bold constructive thoughts, and then the impression of the high-reaching steel skeletons is overpowering. With the raising of the walls, this impression is completely destroyed."[49]

Yet when clad, the frame could evoke not one but a whole series of impressions. William Jordy has pointed out the way the elevations of the Lake Shore Drive apartment buildings change as one moves around them. While this impression of change obviously occurs in the perception of any building, or of any object for that matter, in this case it is heightened by the wide-flange sections and their vertical composition, as well as by the varied profiles of the other parts of the facade. "Change is constant amid these simple things, which—and here is the paradox—are so elemental [primitive] in themselves and in combination that they are intellectually perceived as unchangeable."[50]

Optical effects of this sort were also intended by Berlage, as we have seen. A comparison of Holland House with the rendered facade of Mies's Friedrichstrasse skyscraper reveals surprising similarities: the articulation of repetitive verticals, a weave of dotlike patches of surface, atectonic pattern-making, and synthetic tonal values. It was the idea of the impression, and the subjectivity this implies, that Berlage too advocated, especially in the context of the modern city.

If most of this discussion suggests a comparison to the ISI building, it also indicates a crucial difference: for Venturi and Scott Brown, the primitive or vernacular is traditional, whereas for Berlage and Mies it is industrial. The distinction here is between affirmation of what has been and of what exists now. Both Berlage and Mies argued for "primitive," "natural," and "intrinsic" optics as an inevitable consequence of modernity. The overwhelmingly significant aspect of modernity was industrialization, which Mies, unlike Venturi and Scott Brown, regarded as inescapable and inspiring.

The necessary interconnection between building and culture was demonstrated for Mies in Frobenius's account of "unknown Africa," where the mutuality of a society and its buildings was inescapable. Representation in architecture, for Mies, emerged from the necessities of construction: the availability and economy of materials and techniques, the influence of place, and so on. In

4.14
Ludwig Mies van der Rohe,
Lake Shore Drive apartments,
under construction, Chicago, 1950.

4.15
Ludwig Mies van der Rohe,
Lake Shore Drive apartments,
detail, Chicago, 1951.

"Architecture and Technology," Mies argued that "wherever technology reaches its real fulfillment, it transcends into architecture. It is true that architecture depends on facts, but its real field of activity is in the realm of significance."[51] The "factual" was important, but so too was the "representational." However, the meaning of this latter term must be specified clearly. For Mies, significance in architecture was based on the technology of contemporary methods and materials. In his time, this technology was industrial, which meant that "representation" also must be industrial—presumably not because industrial forms were preferred in themselves, but because the epoch itself was industrial. Yet, however simple and factual such representation may have been, it may not be correct to assume (with Mies) that it was also primitive and natural, in the sense of "unknown Africa." How can the innocence expressed in these "primitive" images be realized when the elements of construction arise from entirely different conditions, namely, mass production?

AESTHETICS IN AN INDUSTRIAL AGE

The wide-flange sections on the exterior of Mies's Lake Shore Drive apartments are non-load-bearing. Mies's critics questioned the purpose of these sections and especially their surface attachment to the metal plates covering the load-bearing steel and concrete piers. In an interview of 1952, Mies offered the following explanation: "It was very important to preserve and extend the rhythm which the mullions set up on the rest of the building. We looked at it on the model without the steel sections attached to the corner columns and it did not look right. That is the real reason. Now [another] reason is that the steel section was needed to stiffen the plate which covers the corner column so this plate would not ripple, and also we needed it for strength when the sections were hoisted into place. Now, of course, that's a very good reason—but the other one is the real reason."[52]

The image for which he was striving, then, was one not of structure but of pattern. Nor is "the nature of materials" expressed; these mullions, like the other parts of the frame, were painted matte black, concealing the color of the steel while also protecting it. Black also gives the buildings a somber quality and a simple or monumental expression, like the figures displayed in the book on unknown Africa. In Mies's later buildings, the use of anodized aluminum would eliminate the need for paint, though this in turn raised questions about the

4.16
Religious building from Sudan and
Bungi region and Yoruba terra-cotta
head, from Leo Frobenius,
Das unbekannte Afrika (1923).

4.17
Ludwig Mies van der Rohe,
alternative design for the Convention
Hall project, Chicago, 1953–1954.
Photo: Hedrich-Blessing.

selection of color. In his earlier buildings, steel columns were clad in chromium, as for example in the Barcelona Pavilion of 1929 and the Tugendhat house of 1930, where the composite character of the columns and the inaccuracies or tolerances of construction are concealed. In each of these cases, and throughout his career, Mies saw a need to cover or clad structural materials. But such cladding, while hiding materials, also reveals the structure, or at least an idealized version of it. Robin Evans has described the structure of the Lake Shore Drive apartments as having the appearance of just hanging there, denying anything to do with heaviness, as if disavowing the force of gravity.[53] The black surfaces of this "idealized" structure also contribute to a sense of lightness by dematerializing the weight they cover. Would it be wrong to call this pattern of weightlessness pure color "appliqué"? Or to compare it to another type of facade on which the surface patterns give the impression of having been cut off before they reach the ground—a facade such as that of Venturi and Scott Brown's Wu Hall? If not, then surely both facades reflect an impressionist approach to cladding. Mies's treatment of the glazing further exemplifies this approach, certainly in his Lake Shore Drive apartments but also in his very early projects for office buildings in Berlin. Although in this sense both early and mature Mies designs can be described as impressionist, they represent an alternative approach to the one taken by Venturi and Scott Brown: the impressionist character of their ISI facade derives from a color pattern permanently inscribed on its surface, whereas the effects produced by light reflecting on the black background of his Berlin and Chicago buildings' cladding result in constantly changing impressions of their facades, as in the case of Berlage's buildings.

IDEALITY OF THE CONSTRUCTED FACT

While conscious of the representational character of his cladding systems, Mies was also aware of buildings that achieved ideality through the pragmatic and utilitarian character of their type and construction methods. One of Mies's better-known photomontages shows a concert hall (1942) set within Albert Kahn's Glenn Martin Bomber Assembly Building of 1937. Kahn's building enclosed an immense single-span, column-free space.[54] Such an open space was required for the manufacture of aircraft—in this case of 250,000-pound flying boats with a wingspan of 300 feet. Mies's choice of this monumental and "dematerialized" setting for a concert hall reflects his preoccupation with open, flexible space, in which he found opportunities for the realization of this type, using props that were, as he often put it, *beinahe nichts* or "next to nothing." The fact that this concert hall design was developed as a montage, by surgically inserting performance "props" into a photograph, suggests the importance he attached to material "facts" in the development of his designs and his willingness to appropriate a ready-made setting as a site of architectural invention. Yet the inserts in the montage also cover the structure of the building, masking or dressing it, as does the cladding on the columns of the Lake Shore Drive apartments, but only partially, for while the structure and the space are overlapped, we can still see bomber wings, clerestory lights, and roof trusses. The presence of the bombers in the space of the montage suggests a potentially surreal meeting between these war machines and the statue of a peaceful and melancholic female figure in the foreground of one version of this study.

Other factory interiors could have been chosen. Why this one? If not surreal, the juxtaposition is at least ironic. Randall Ott has explained that Mies together with his assistants and students made several versions of this collage. One version shows an Egyptian Old Kingdom sculpture, another—the version shown here—a sculpture by Maillol. The figures are predominantly non-Western.[55] Regardless of thematic content, this is an architecture of contrasts, in which opaque and disconnected walls and ceilings float in a lightweight, transparent, and totalized container. The juxtaposition of opposites is also apparent in the use of material: a thin curved wall of polished marble contrasts with the repetitive and industrialized steel structure. The insertion of opaque surfaces and the figure in the foreground renders the transparency of the perimeter cladding even more vivid—as if transparency results from opacity.

To see this as true, we would have to reconsider transparency. We normally think of it as a spatial condition that involves either actually "seeing through" architectural elements or virtually doing so. We have come to accept the definitions of "literal" and "phenomenal" transparency developed by Colin Rowe and Robert Slutzky in their well-known article of 1963.[56] In neither category does opacity figure prominently. Nor, for that matter, does it seem apposite to the sort of contemporary architecture that uncritically adopts the polemical distinction between outside and inside. Our contemporary "architecture of fragments" arises from a sense of architecture in which any separation between inside and outside is greatly reduced or eliminated, allowing each to pass into the other and the emergence of a thoroughgoing "openness." Yet Mies's concert hall project seems

4.18
Ludwig Mies van der Rohe,
project for a concert hall, 1942.

to suggest a significant role for opaque forms and figures, as do the other buildings we have examined. Is it not the case that the opaque elements are the very ones that allow for the perception of spatial depth and continuity from inside to outside? In the absence of any overlap between the two, would there be any sense of depth in this setting? Occlusion would seem to be important and perhaps essential to spatial continuity, presuming the layering or overlapping of both hidden and visible elements. The problem with X-ray vision is that it takes for granted, but cannot explain, the constitution of a spatial continuum. The territory between a foreground and a background figure is an element of both separation and connection, the place where one passes into or onto the next. In Mies's concert hall collage, the tension between the foreground figure and the bomber in the background defines both the boundary of the building's interior (across the dark, then light floor plane) and its "openness" into or onto the surrounding field (the one from which we view the interior and the one that admits light from the rear). Stating that transparency results from opacity suggests that elements which resist X-ray penetration are the real basis of seeing through and seeing beyond, whether they are thick or thin. Without elements such as these, there would be neither a through nor a beyond because one's position "here," as distinct from "there," could not be established. In fact, the play of light and reflection proposed in arguments about "sliding surfaces," "chromatic radiance," and "weightless structure" takes for granted the existence of surfaces with characteristics that are opposite to those of light, that is, materials that have these properties precisely because they are opaque. This is what Voysey, Berlage, Fabiani, and the others knew when they chose to use opaque surfaces to define streets and interiors.

ARCHITECTURE FOR INDUSTRY

Mies's appropriation of the Martin bomber factory as a ready-made setting differs from Kahn's own intentions in developing the building. While "open" as an interior, the vast space was for Kahn specifically determined by the pragmatic necessities of producing 300-foot-wide airplanes. Also important in determining the building's simplicity was the speed of its construction: "Speed and more speed is the watchword. . . . There [is] no time for philosophizing, waiting for inspiration, or even considering the matter of aesthetics. . . . Simplicity of design and construction are imperative. Every day counts and minutes must be saved. It is not only a matter of dollars and cents but [is], today, a matter of life and death."[57] Producing buildings was like producing war planes; speed and economy of means demanded a clear understanding of the task at hand in order to prevent waste and redundancy. Later, the same came to be true for the production of automobiles. Speed and economy were achieved by determining as exactly as possible the purposes to be fulfilled by the building. In factories, this "purpose" was flexibility. Such was not the purpose of all building types, Kahn thought—and this is where he differed with an architect such as Mies, but also with Le Corbusier and others—nor was flexibility the purpose of all spaces within the factory.

To begin to understand this, it will be useful to compare the entry with the manufacturing space in one of Kahn's buildings. The Lady Esther factory in Clearing, Illinois, for example, has an entry lobby enclosed by a glass block wall, stylized surface treatment, and appropriate furnishings—all meant to be "bright and cheerful." This Art Deco architecture contrasts with the utilitarian manufacturing space, which is qualified by a highly polished floor and uniform lighting. If the first can be described as an image of a modern factory, the second can be described as its actual realization.

The uniformity of lighting in the manufacturing space results from both ceiling and perimeter glazing. The originality of this kind of illumination can be seen clearly when a space for mass production is contrasted with one for "static assembly." In the former case, as represented by Kahn's Half-Ton Truck Plant in Detroit, the horizontal expanse of perimeter glazing parallels—and even mirrors—the extension of the assembly line. In a space for static assembly, by contrast, each manufacturing table is positioned next to an individual opening in the perimeter wall. Likewise, in traditional load-bearing wall construction, glazing was limited to a maximum of 50 percent of the perimeter wall,[58] because the wood-beam floor construction and the arched heads of the windows reduced the potential area for glazing near the ceiling, where windows would have been most valuable. Further, projecting beams and load-bearing columns on the interior prevented the maximum penetration of light. In contrast to earlier modes of load-bearing, reinforced concrete and steel construction allowed for up to 80 percent of the wall to be used for glazing by reducing wall columns to minimum width and window jambs to minimum depth. These types of construction also allowed beams to be placed above rather than below the ceiling, allowing ideal lighting conditions. Such innovations were especially important in multifloor buildings. Furthermore, with mushroom column construction, supports at the perimeter of

4.19
Albert Kahn, Lady Esther factory,
lobby, Clearing, Illinois, 1936.

the building were no longer necessary. Floor slabs were cantilevered beyond the points of support, which were withdrawn toward the inside, with the result that the window area could be increased up to 100 percent. Other types of cantilever could also free up the perimeter. This building system, together with the degree of illumination it allowed, served as the setting for the development of mass production.

The correspondence between building construction and its purpose is perhaps most evident in the use of standardized metal windows in these early factory buildings, for they both allowed for mass production and resulted from it. In the Lady Esther factory building, the exterior skin that encloses the manufacturing space is uninterrupted by load-bearing elements. The building's overall length is determined by the extent of straight-line production, which is in principle limitless. This characteristic of the factory's functioning resulted from the idea that the entire plant should be enclosed under one roof. In fact, this idea was not new at this time; factory builders in the nineteenth century also envisaged this goal. Its realization in Kahn's buildings, however, resulted in buildings that could be indefinitely extended without interrupting production. In the external enclosure of this type of "extendable" space, the wall as an instrument of load-bearing soon disappeared, as did the window as an obviously distinct unit; windows were still there, but largely hidden or absorbed into the regular pattern of modules that extended across the wall's length, resulting in a uniformity of appearance. This development signaled the birth of the window wall, a type of cladding that dissolved differences between architectural elements, as we have shown in the preceding chapter. The dissolution of differences between architectural elements seems to work together with the limitless character of straight-line production and the uniformity of lighting.

Not only was the quantity of lighting important in these factories but also its quality. To be of the most value, lighting had to be as uniform as possible during all working hours, a requirement achieved most effectively through artificial lighting. In single-story buildings, the use of sawtooth skylights often accomplished this purpose. By means of these elements, uniform lighting existed in most of Kahn's factories.

In describing the spatial character of Kahn's buildings, his contemporaries introduced an aquatic or electrical metaphor: the space, like the assembly process and the daylight, was meant to "flow" without interruption: continuously, continually, and rapidly. This metaphor can be made more concrete when the

4.20
Albert Kahn, Lady Esther factory,
exterior, Clearing, Illinois, 1936.

"flow" of production is related to the organization of labor and the movement of capital: all restrictions that reduced likely gain or increase were to be eliminated. Yet equally significant, and more specific, is the impact this style of thinking had on Kahn's architectural practice. For his association with the Ford Company, he was required to modify his practice in order to become part of the production team, devoted to the "reproduction of mass production."[59] This new style of practice was illustrated in a chart of the Kahn firm's organization, published in George Nelson's book on Kahn's architecture, the principal tenet of which was completeness of services rendered.[60] The uniqueness of this organization can be seen by comparison to one proposed by Richard Neutra, which he described in a similar diagram published nine years earlier in his study of American building practices. Neutra envisaged an organization in which everyone in the firm would be subordinated to the architect. On Nelson's chart, by contrast, the chief administrator was superior.[61] Just as industry embraced architecture in Kahn's company, so the practice of design embraced industrialized organization. Nelson observed that individuals like Henry Ford wanted to deal with businessmen when planning their buildings: "they were profoundly suspicious of artists, [for] they wanted fast work, and no mistakes." Similarly, Kahn asserted: "Architecture is 90 percent business and 10 percent art." And this meant that the work in the office had to be organized, efficient, and systematic. In the 1930s and 1940s, there were twenty to thirty buildings going through the organization at any given time. In order for the work to flow through its various stages as smoothly as the product "flows" through the factory itself, office practices had to be standardized. Just as Kahn brought architecture to industry, he brought industry to architecture.

For Knud Lönberg-Holm, who wrote three decades later and was employed by the Dodge Corporation to redesign the *Sweet's* Catalog, all sorts of human endeavor were meant to "flow": workers in a factory, cars on highways, information across a page, and pedestrian movement through space.[62] In 1947 George Howe had also widely applied the aquatic metaphor: "All is now flux in very fact: flow of traffic, flow of production, flow of people. Two faced Janus, god of the threshold and monumental steps, has been banished . . . giving way to ideal space, invisible, mysterious."[63]

Buildings that resulted from this flowing sort of organization both utilized the techniques of mass production and arose from the circumstances of that production, as we have seen in the case of the window wall enclosing the space of

ORGANIZATION

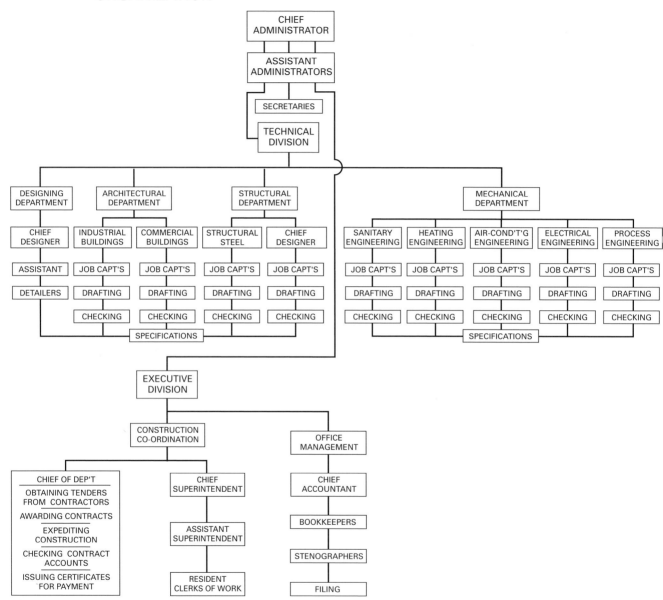

4.21

Organization of Albert Kahn, Inc.,
from George Nelson, *Industrial
Architecture of Albert Kahn, Inc.* (1939).

straight-line production. For Albert Kahn, other circumstances—those of a house or concert hall, for example—gave rise to other kinds of architecture. At the end of his career, reflecting on the whole of his architectural practice, Kahn asserted that his favorite building was the Clements Library at the University of Michigan (1920–1921), which could be mistaken for Vignola's casino for the Villa Farnese at Caprarola. (Kahn may have seen Vignola's building in 1919.) Or, again, his design may recall a similar design by McKim, Mead and White. In either case, the library is an example of an architecture of recollection, rather than one resulting from contemporary circumstances of production.

This suggests that there are two sorts of architecture for two sorts of use programs. This seems to have been Kahn's position: architecture is distinct from building, as we elaborated earlier. Yet Kahn's apologist, George Nelson, disagreed with this distinction between various architectural tasks, despite his genuine praise of Kahn's work as a whole. He described Kahn's factories as examples of the most significant architectural achievements of the time, even though they were "useful" buildings. Nelson thought the factories disproved the nineteenth-century assumption that "art [or architecture] is not art unless it is useless." He would also have disagreed with Walter Gropius, who said architecture begins where engineering ends. Innovations in factory production and factory building led to innovations in architecture. While critics of the time may have regretted the absence of "design" in these buildings, Nelson thought they exhibited an extraordinary purity of form and that in these buildings modern architecture had reached its most complete expression. The most striking example is, perhaps, the Half-Ton Truck building, a building that encloses nearly half a million square feet and yet was built in eighty-one days.

In the Half-Ton Truck building, the organization of work and the organization of the plan are virtually identical. The drawings of this and similar buildings convey what must be known for the purposes of construction (not appearance) as it must unfold as a process. The buildings that resulted were, in ways that were unprecedented, largely *nonvisual*. Flexibility required emptiness, which explains why "almost nothing" exists in plan. But neither is there anything to be seen or to look at, as there clearly was in Mies's buildings. This is an instance of production *as* representation. One can say such a building is nothing more than an "assembly of its purposes, the movement of its machines, the spaces in which materials are stored and in which jobs are done."[64] For some critics, this was an especially American cultural condition, one that arose out of new forms of labor. Antonio Gramsci, for example, writing in his *Prison Notebooks,* described how "in the new 'Fordized' man the active use of at least some intelligence, fantasy, and initiative in professional work is broken by redefining work as physical, mechanical exclusively. The mental and the imaginative are split two ways: at the plant they become the preserve of management, and within the New Man they are placed in abeyance until he goes home."[65] This split is also evident in Kahn's architecture. Compare again the University of Michigan library or any one of his civic buildings with the factories: the former is the domain of "intelligence," symbolism, and significance, while the latter is the site of physical work, pragmatism, and rationalized processes. The two types of architecture also display different attitudes toward historical time: the first comes out of the past, the archive; the second is of the present, off the assembly line. The same difference exists between the fronts of the factory buildings, where the offices for management are located, and the backs, which contain the spaces for production and laborers. Two sorts of functionalism can be distinguished: the "nothing but" functionalism of the backs and the "image of" function in the Art Deco stylizing of the fronts, as in the Lady Esther Factory. Distinctions between uses and corresponding degrees of power explain the strong difference between the "look" of these two sorts of architecture. The production spaces lack an intended appearance other than the "look" that resulted from the rationalized processes of the building's production—production as representation. For Kahn, pragmatic simplicity was key; he argued for neither aesthetic functionalism nor the "shaven architecture" of the European modernists, whom he strongly criticized for having taken functionalism to the nth degree. His disagreement was also political and economic; he ended a lecture on modern architecture by recognizing the need for architects to pursue the model of corporate management, integrating architecture with the business of building.[66]

These factories are not, however, without aesthetic quality. Despite his admiration for historical architecture, Kahn himself was aware of this; after reasserting the need to eliminate nonessentials, and making comparisons to the "fitness to purpose," quality, and *beauty* of modern airplanes, he wrote: "The frank expression of the functional, the structural, element of the industrial building makes for success."[67] In contemporary photographs, one gets the sense of a potent stillness, a limpid weave of light and lightweight elements, which serves to provide potential energy for the organized arena of work spread across the floor surface. Perhaps it is helpful to recall images of the interiors of large railway terminals, with the calm luminous ceiling space floating above the rushing crowd below. Is this not the strong sense of the "nearly nothing" that Mies envisaged, an emptiness that is full of continuous but enclosed light: not a lack, but a potential?

FACTORY-MADE

Another reason for the empty quality of the buildings and the drawings designed for their construction is that they relied upon the existence and availability of factory-made elements of assembly. On existing plans of the Martin Assembly Building, for example, the trusses are drawn with single lines only, diagramming length, position, and shape but not specifying other characteristics, such as materials or thicknesses. This lack of specification is not because these characteristics were unknown, but rather because they were known so well, if not by the architect then by the engineer, who was authoritative in specifying the sizing of elements (then as now). The cooperation between the manufacturers of architectural elements and the architects themselves is apparent when one reads the contemporary professional periodicals such as *Architectural Forum*. The same realization led George Nelson to observe that "what was known as 'factory building' in the last century has become 'industrial architecture' today."[68] Window manufacturers in the 1930s often illustrated their products with perspective drawings or photographs of buildings by Albert Kahn. These drawings have the same diagrammatic quality as the plans and sections in Kahn's published drawings.

Site work for such a building consists of assembly, the economic incentives of which are clear: the fabrication of ready-made parts in dry construction proceeds more rapidly than on-site wet construction. But another aspect of this manner of working is significant: both design and site work have been transformed into a process of *assemblage*. We have already discussed the use of montage in the design work of Mies van der Rohe. This process was, however, anticipated in areas of work that did not intend aesthetic objects. Their procedures were, nonetheless, analogically similar to those used in montage—both involved the juxtaposition of elements.[69]

In his assemblage of a factory, Kahn paid no attention to the metaphoric potential of juxtaposition; instead, he concentrated on factual assembly. Although presumably unintended by Kahn, this, too, had its parallel in contemporary art, notably in the attention to *faktura* in Soviet avant-garde art from as early as 1912,

4.22

Gustav Klutsis, *Struggle for Heat
and Metal,* 1933. Courtesy of the Russia
State Library, Moscow.

as expressed in the writings of Mikhail Larionov, for example.[70] A contrast with traditional pictorial practice is instructive: "Quite unlike the traditional idea of *fattura* or *facture* in painting, where the masterful facture of a painter's hand spiritualizes the mere materiality of the pictorial production, and where the hand becomes at the same time the substitute or the totalization of the identifying signature . . . the new concern for *faktura* in the Soviet avant-garde emphasizes precisely the mechanical quality, the materiality, and the anonymity of the painterly procedure from a perspective of empirico-critical positivism . . . it demystifies claims to authenticity."[71] The same emphasis on mechanical quality, "mere" materiality, and "empirico-critical positivism" exists in these "assembled" factory buildings: factory as *faktura*. It is important to note that in Soviet society this practice of making was entirely congenial to the organization of labor, as it was in America. Even if Kahn did not intend parallels with this aesthetic theory, he did propose correspondences with Fordism and Taylorism.[72] He also designed hundreds of plants for Soviet engineers, having established a special office with 1,500 draftsmen in Moscow after receiving an order in 1928 for a four-million-dollar tractor plant near Stalingrad.

While the principle of simplicity allows us to grasp the conformity of this kind of architecture to the methods of mass production, another tenet of factory production in the first decades of the twentieth century is equally important: that of economy through speed. We have already observed the importance of speed in assembly processes on a dry site. For the leaders of the Austin Company, one of Kahn's competitors, "economy through speed" became a guiding axiom of building production.

At the outset of World War I, rapidity of production was the most important factor in building. Designs were standardized, but so were elements of construction. To control this process, the Austin Company moved away from the practice of storing structural steel (steel that had been made to order) to a practice of actually fabricating building parts in its own workshops. This change allowed the company to reduce the time for assembling a large factory building to under sixty days. These methods could also be applied to the fabrication of railways and railway buildings; in fact, this style of factory building was an outgrowth of railway production, itself dating from the mid-nineteenth century. Many of the factory buildings by both Kahn and the Austin Company recall the typology of the railway terminal, with its front (civic) facade and its linear and extended rear shed, invariably made of steel and glass. Often the factories were sited alongside or as the terminus to railway lines, allowing for the continuous "flow" of raw material into the factory and of finished products to sales and distribution centers.

We have already compared the lighting of a Kahn factory to the interior space of railway terminals. Sigfried Giedion described the same quality of lighting in the glass-covered interior of Paxton's Crystal Palace, which he compared to the luminous spaces of Turner's paintings: "[Turner's *Simplon Pass*] uses a humid atmosphere to dematerialize landscape and dissolve it into infinity. The Crystal Palace realizes the same intention through the agency of transparent surfaces and iron structural members. In the Turner picture the means employed are less abstract, but an equivalent insubstantial and hovering effect is produced."[73] Dematerialization and transparency resulted in the creation of a spatial quality that was both unlimited and weightless: ferrovitreous construction dissolving itself into infinity, where "all materiality blends into the atmosphere."

It seems fair to observe that Kahn would have argued that a spatial quality such as this was appropriate for some but not all building types. In his criticism of the International Style generally and the work of Le Corbusier specifically, he characterized an architecture of transparent screens, unadorned surfaces, and simple volumes as tedious and monotonous: "It would be sad indeed if an International Style based upon [the theories of the modernists] became a reality. Imagine not only a city but many lands building in accordance with one formula, and that applied [to all types]."[74] An architecture that neglected type differences and regional characteristics was the opposite of what he desired. Kahn's interest in regional particularity led him to envisage an American architecture, something, he observed, that neither Sullivan nor Wright had accomplished. But it was even more important to preserve a differentiation of types against the influence of International Style modernism. The qualities of his factories—much appreciated by modern architects, and by Hitchcock and Johnson—were not to be those of other types, Kahn thought: "I can see a very close analogy between the modern industrial building and the modern box-like, flat roofed house, so many of which are erected today. At that, while I admire many of the modern factories, I can't say as much for many of these houses. Indeed, much already done and being done under so-called modernism, is to me extremely ugly and monotonous. . . . A building to be good, even today, must express its purpose and look like it is."[75] Houses must look like houses, theaters like theaters, and factories like factories. The principle is clear, but problematic; for the appearances of the first two often cover the materials that give the building its durable support, while those of the third—the factories for which Kahn was so famous—did not. Kahn's acceptance of type differences, based on historical associations with traditional uses, prevented him from envisaging the prospect of "an architecture," a manner of building in which the claims of appearance would be met by the opportunities of production—exactly what had been proposed, although never realized, in modernism.

THE LIGHT OF INDUSTRY

Good lighting was a characteristic of much of Albert Kahn's factory architecture, because it served as a necessary condition for the performance of productive work and maximized efficiency, ensuring effective management. Nevertheless, it did not necessarily provide for humane working conditions, let alone the architectural expression of symbolic values, which had for centuries been one of the functions of lighting. Further, while Kahn's factory buildings as well as those of the Austin Company developed many important technical advances, they were also the source of some criticism. An instructive case is contained in the documents relating to the van Nelle factory, built in Rotterdam in the 1920s under the direction of C. H. van der Leeuw, industrialist, philanthropist, and architectural enthusiast. Reporting on one of his visits to the United States, van der Leeuw criticized the treatment of the workforce as well as the effect of the buildings' construction on workers. He faulted the broad expanse of the manufacturing space for preventing natural light from entering the middle section of the floor, with the result that some working areas depended on artificial light all day long. He also criticized the use of mercury tubular lamps, which produced a disagreeable blue daylight color. Lastly, he regretted the crowded working conditions which had an adverse effect on the quality of air. None of these conditions, he observed, would be accepted by the labor inspectorate in the Netherlands.[1] However, van der Leeuw's criticism of these buildings did not prevent him from utilizing many of the advances they represented, particularly the electric lighting system of the Nela Park factory, the home office of Lampworks of General Electric Company.

Van der Leeuw's appreciation of this building was not limited to concern for management and efficiency of labor; equally strong was his interest in both the well-being of those who spent a large part of their lives in the factory and what one might call the spiritual significance of the lighting. Van der Leeuw was a member of the Order of the Star of the East, a theosophic society that counted Annie Besant and Jiddu Krishnamurti among its members. His theosophic beliefs, like theirs, were based on a knowledge of nature taken to be more profound than that obtained from empirical science alone. Besant, Krishnamurti, and Madame Blavatsky, the leaders of the movement, held that this knowledge would serve as the basis for a universal brotherhood of man. While this philanthropic aspiration might seem opposed to an empirico-scientific attitude, both coexisted in van der Leeuw's mind. For this reason, his theosophy was complemented by his American experience. Lighting, for example, could introduce both the pragmatic and symbolic dimensions of interior space.

The quality of lighting in the van Nelle factory resulted from a construction and glazing system similar to what we have seen in Kahn's factories. One obvious difference is that the building in Rotterdam is supported by a concrete rather than a steel frame and is multistory. But as in the American example of load-bearing concrete frame structures, the octagonal columns of the van Nelle building are capped with mushroom heads to support perimeter cantilevers and to maximize the open space within, while freeing the ceiling plane from beams and secondary structure.[2] The surface of the interior walls is covered with a German plaster and impregnated with quartz fragments that reflect the sun brilliantly. On the exterior, the glazing spans the entire length of the facades and covers the whole height from each floor to the next, apart from the area covered by a low wall. When originally built, the cladding formed a uniform, flat surface and had operable windows at regular intervals. Since then, an exterior screening system has been added to the windows on the building's office wing. Two other clear differences between this building and any one of Kahn's factories are its verticality and its conformity to the site. In the American factories, a principle of unlimited expansion allowed the buildings to extend onto the land as far as the straight-line assembly processes required; by contrast, parts of the van Nelle building have been formed into separate wings (of eight, six, and three stories),

5.1

Johannes Brinkman, Mart Stam, et al.,
van Nelle factory, Rotterdam, 1930.
Photo: Charles H. Tashima, 1991.

while the office space has formed its own wing, curving away from the river toward a street at an oblique angle.

Special attention was paid to the availability of building materials for the outside of the building. The original design of the main facade, for example, was changed from five horizontal panes to a vertical arrangement with only one horizontal member in order to accommodate common glass measurements. These vertical windows were combined with panels made of steel plate with a "torfoleum" isolation in between. These panels, in combination with the windows, cover a whole floor of the building, forming a perfectly uniform curtain wall. Its design recalls the cladding of the Bauhaus building constructed in 1926. Van der Vlugt, the main architect of the van Nelle project, visited the Bauhaus and is known to have been on friendly terms with Gropius. In addition, Mart Stam, a collaborator on the project, had close ties with the avant-garde circle of the architects responsible for the experimental projects of the Weissenhofsiedlung in Stuttgart.

Unlike the factories of Albert Kahn, which were primarily designed to accommodate the rationalized processes of manufacture, the van Nelle factory had as its task a collaborative and communitarian project with its roots in van der Leeuw's theosophic and humanistic ideals. The ultimate failure of the project's utopic and social ambitions has not undermined the importance of the building as one of modernism's more unconventional icons. The van Nelle factory was an important amalgam of American pragmatism in the field of industrialization and European idealism. American methods of production had a more general influence in the Netherlands, however, particularly on the group of architects associated with the so-called Nieuwe Bouwen.

Experimentation with new materials and techniques of production was a chief concern of these architects. Their interest in standardization, in combination with a building's function, could result in a "tailor-made" architecture. The use of standard building elements made it possible to replace parts of the building in response to temporal changes in function.[3] This attitude, though reminiscent of American ideas about Taylorization, was nevertheless used differently in the van Nelle and Kahn factories.

Because speed was necessary for both the construction of American factories and their actual use, what the buildings looked like was not important but rather how they functioned as sites of production. The van Nelle factory, on the other hand, despite the Nieuwe Bouwen group's interest in rationalized systems

of production, was a unique building. Its architects produced numerous compositional schemes and many three-dimensional representations, including perspectives, all intended to convey the building's appearance. Whereas for Kahn the Art Deco facade of the office building was the only instance of representation that was thought to be necessary, the Dutch architects thought that the whole ensemble served purposes of signification. As a consequence, in the van Nelle building there is no major distinction between the architecture of the factory and that of the office; all of its parts are "architecture," which means that none of them (such as the "rear") is mere building. Exterior and interior qualities of the building's cladding, especially the natural lighting of the interior through the building's transparent and industrially produced skin, provide its visual identity and style. The van Nelle factory is as much a site of production as it is a monument visibly demonstrating the humanitarian benevolence and patronage of its owners.

MODERN APPEARANCES AND PRACTICALITY

This same synthesis between industrialized and tailor-made architectural elements can be found in the most important example of American office construction of this period: the PSFS building by George Howe and William Lescaze, built in Philadelphia between 1929 and 1932.[4] While its importance cannot be denied, the building has been neglected somewhat in the history of modern architecture, partly because it has been placed in an awkward age of the movement. According to Frederick Gutheim, it was "not new enough to be contemporary" and "not old enough to have become a readily placed historical monument." Furthermore, the building still carries traces of the earlier Beaux-Arts tradition of design, despite its prominent position in Hitchcock and Johnson's *The International Style* of 1932. And while the building was seen by many to be ultramodern, its owner understood its design to result from practical considerations. Practicality was wedded to a look that expressed progressive thinking. The same coupling of tradition and modernity can be seen in the relationship between the building's two architects: Howe represented the best of the tradition; Lescaze brought to the project the momentum of European modernism. Both were necessary in dealing with the client, who was himself a product of traditional values but also aware that cultural conditions were no longer the same.

The PSFS building was designed to be "ultra practical." This term can be understood in two senses, programmatic and technological. Under the heading

5.2
George Howe and William Lescaze,
Philadelphia Savings Fund Society
building, Philadelphia, 1932.
Photo: Carlos Naranjo, 2000.

5.3
George Howe and William Lescaze,
Philadelphia Savings Fund Society
building, Philadelphia, 1932.

of programmatic practicality, much has been written about the novelty and intelligence of placing the commercial and public banking facilities on the building's second floor, above street level. While controversial because uncommon, this decision proved to have great practical advantage, freeing the ground level for retail activities, which attracted into the bank potential customers who might not otherwise have entered the building. This aspect of the design might be described as practical urbanism. The building's practicality is also architectural, however, as is apparent in its distribution of interior settings and the elements that accommodate their use—those that provide for daylighting, for example, but also its thermal environment and its furnishings. These characteristics were as much the result of the asymmetrical additive arrangement of the building's overall volumes, responding to local site conditions, as of its equipment and mechanical parts. (The PSFS building was the second high-rise in the United States to be fully air conditioned.) Program and use were not made to conform to the logic of an idealized structural frame but were taken as the basis for differentiating pragmatically determined volumes. While compromising its formal ideality, this attention to particularity of site and use supported the practicality prized by its owner, architects, and apologists.

Apart from responding to the circumstantial conditions of the site—setbacks, planning codes, etc.—the asymmetrical logic of the building's configuration was legitimized by the architects with reference to both ancient and modern precedents: the buildings of the Acropolis were invoked as examples of such a balance between independent and nonsymmetrical parts, as was Le Corbusier's praise for this sort of massing in *Vers une architecture* of 1923. Explaining the project, Howe stated: "The soundest precedents for such asymmetries are to be found in the grouping of numerous buildings in Greek architecture, as on the Acropolis, for a modern building is really a group of many smaller buildings. While thinking always in terms of utility and economic soundness we have constantly kept architectural effect in view and by a logical and reasoned use of the elements natural to a business building have produced an irregular and organic mass of impressive effect."[5] On this point Howe has drawn an exact parallel with Le Corbusier's explanation of the asymmetry of the Acropolis: "Set on its rock and on its sustaining walls, seen from afar, [it] appears as one solid block. The buildings are massed together in accordance with the incidents of the varying plans."[6] This concern for the building's overall appearance is also similar to the concerns

5.4
George Howe and William Lescaze,
Philadelphia Savings Fund Society
building, banking room, Philadelphia,
1932.

expressed by the architects of the van Nelle factory, a concern Albert Kahn neglected.

The asymmetry of the PSFS building was made possible through a number of unusual engineering designs. Purdy and Henderson, the consulting structural engineers, referred to three: (1) the extensive use of knee bracing for wind resistance, (2) the use of cantilevered construction, and (3) the unusual placement of columns in relation to the building's outer walls. The impressive expanse and uniform luminosity of the famous banking room were made possible by a very large transfer structure, hidden behind the ceiling and external cladding. Original or unusual as these designs were, little of the building's engineering is actually visible beneath the surface coverings, which resulted from other requirements—those of the site (code requirements, patterns of use, etc.) and of composition and appearance. Could this mode of working be called collage because it involves assembly of independent figures? Could it, then, be identified with Mies's method? The fact that the structure is covered would suggest that the answer to both questions is no, that this building is as close to buildings of the Beaux-Arts—which also covered structure with aesthetically determined coverings—as it is to Miesian construction before and after the war. Put differently, is it possible that the building is somehow caught between these two alternatives, neither modern nor traditional, as Gutheim observed? Describing his conversion to functionalism, George Howe explained that the practical and technological requirements of the bank led him to reject his "stone-age ideal" of solid masonry walls and to embrace frame-and-cladding wall construction, but not for purposes of concealment nor to allow for "tatooed skin treatment"; instead, "skeleton, organs of circulation, respiration . . . sheathed in only a thin outer skin" would serve the essentially architectural purpose of reconciling "material order" with "emotional intensity."[7]

The building's exterior had to respond to local codes and regulations just as its interior had to respond to the bank's program. For example, brick was used on the spandrel panels, throughout the full height of the tower, because building codes prohibited the use of metal for this purpose. Nevertheless, the building achieved its modern appearance through the use of flush glazing on the lower levels, aluminum for the window frames, and the highly polished charcoal-colored granite that covers the base. The use of aluminum and granite on the outside, like that of stainless steel and marble on the inside, was as much a function of practicality as of appearance. Bought inexpensively at the outset of the

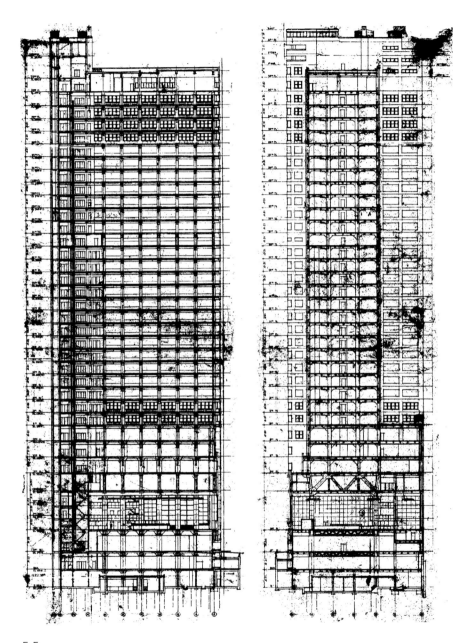

5.5

George Howe and William Lescaze,
Philadelphia Savings Fund Society
building, structural section,
Philadelphia, 1932.

Depression, these materials, which would have been prohibitively expensive at any other time, contributed to long-term savings on maintenance costs, while they—or the way they were detailed—contributed to the building's modern appearance.

When the PSFS building was being built, more and more elements of architectural construction were designed to be shop-fabricated. This represents an important change in the logic of building production, pointing toward the industrialization not only of the parts of a building but of the building itself. Further, it points to a change from construction as site work to construction as *installation* of elements made away from the site, sometimes in a factory but most often in a shop. Although this change recalls the construction procedure of buildings by both Albert Kahn and the Austin Company, the construction process of the PSFS building was different; in a word, it was stylized.

Many historians have identified formal precedents for the PSFS building, in most cases precedents from European modernists, often émigrés, like Lescaze himself. Two cases in point are Erich Mendelsohn and Richard Neutra. Mendelsohn's Berliner Tageblatt (1923), Schocken Department Store in Stuttgart (1926), and Universum Cinema in Berlin (1926–1929) are relevant examples, as is Neutra's office building for his Rush City Reformed project of 1926–1927. In a number of ways, Neutra seems to be the key figure. He claimed a significant role in Mendelsohn's designs while he worked in his office, and an especially influential role in the design of the Tageblatt building. Particularly relevant to Lescaze's design, however, is Neutra's Rush City office building and store project, for it, like the PSFS building, has a three-story base that follows the alignment of its streets and sidewalks, and a tower above that is set back from the street frontage. The articulation of this volume reflects the difference between principal and secondary streets, with the contrast between horizontal banding on the narrow facade and vertical elements on the long facade, similar to the composition of the PSFS building. The corner of the lower volume on the PSFS building is curved in a way that recalls the buildings of Mendelsohn but also Neutra's National Trading Center project (c. 1929). Lescaze himself seems to have been concerned with curved and cantilevered urban corners before the PSFS design, as is demonstrated by his Capital Bus Terminal in New York of 1927. This latter building has also been compared to J. J. P. Oud's Kiefhoek housing estate in Rotterdam.

The wealth of visual references for the PSFS building confirms that its design was not totally original. It has the look of the modern (European) projects of the time, which seems to be the main reason Hitchcock and Johnson included it in the International Style exhibition. At the same time, it was the sole built exemplar of the genre in the United States. The collaboration between Howe the converted modernist and Lescaze, who was educated at the ETH in Zurich under Karl Moser, meant that this building was an opportunity to actually work out the tenets of modern architecture throughout all of its parts and its technology; and this is what its architects did, making the design essentially different from the technique of covering a traditional building with images of modern architecture. At the same time, great attention was also paid to the circumstances of the program (banking) and the building's urban location (in central Philadelphia), which led to the praise we have already observed of its "ultra practicality." In this, the architects seem to have had little choice, for their client was a businessman whose commitments to market success were as strong as they were to architectural modernism, whatever that might have meant for him. The raised banking floor, the air conditioning, the mixed-use program, and so on were characteristics of a new type for the bank, which made the project uncertain in its outcome but also modern (that is, contemporary). Thus, far from being little more than an *image* of modernism or a visualization of its tenets only, the building was also modern because it acknowledged contemporary conditions of life. Put simply, it was modern because of both its appearance and the inventive way it interpreted its particular program and place.

PREFABRICATION AND PERSONALITY

While the PSFS building was doubtless the most famous large-scale building of its time to utilize as many prefabricated components as possible, it was far from the only building to attempt this. Likewise, its architects were not the only ones of this era to see the importance of embracing modern methods of construction. Other European émigrés to the States represented this aspect of modernism too. Perhaps the most useful of the group to consider is Richard Neutra, whose writings and projects demonstrate very clearly the difficulty and promise of industrialized building, especially as concerns the outer covering and appearance of buildings.

In 1927 Neutra, who had been a student of Adolf Loos and of Max Fabiani, published *Wie baut Amerika*. Widely read throughout Europe, America, and even Japan, this book contained photographs of American buildings (designed by Gill, Wright, and Schindler) and building practices (in Chicago especially), together with Neutra's own urban designs and projects for prefabricated houses. While one-third of the book argued for a new urbanism (which included the Rush City Reformed project), and another third presented a detailed account of contemporary American building practices (describing specifically the Palmer Hotel in Chicago, on which Neutra worked when employed by Holabird and Roche), the last section of the book presented examples of recent American architecture and contained arguments concerning the standardization of building components. Some of the final images in the book were of pueblo buildings in Taos, New Mexico, which also exhibited standardization—or so Neutra thought—but not industrialization; thus he cited their relevance to modern times, despite their premodern materials and production methods.

In this last section of the book, Neutra also presented his designs for a prefabricated house, designs that proposed a multiphased scheme to accommodate a growing family. This new type was to have been built out of prefabricated elements. Throughout the early decades of his career, Neutra elaborated versions of this panel; in later formulations, the panels were made of steam-hardened "diatomaceous earth," a kind of earth he said was in great abundance in California. These panels, patented by Neutra's brother and invented by an Austrian chemist, were recommended for use because they were highly effective as insulation and lightweight but could be reinforced with steel and prefinished. Neutra called them Diatom panels and used this name for the house that was to result from their use. Although the Fuller-like, tensile-structure design was never built, the panel itself seems to have received some attention.[8] Already by 1923 he had prepared many details demonstrating how elements of this kind, fabricated elsewhere, could be connected to or "plugged into" a site that had been plumbed prior to their arrival. Neutra continued to publish designs for Diatom houses into the 1930s and 1940s. He also developed new technologies for placing standardized constructions on their sites—the aspect of construction that had traditionally involved building foundation walls. His system involved the use of both shop-built footings and adjustable metal foundations that would allow the prefabricated components to be assembled on any site without interrupting the flow of the natural terrain, thus suiting varying conditions of soil and grade. This dedication to prefabrication was

5.6
Richard Neutra,
office building project,
from *Wie baut Amerika* (1927).

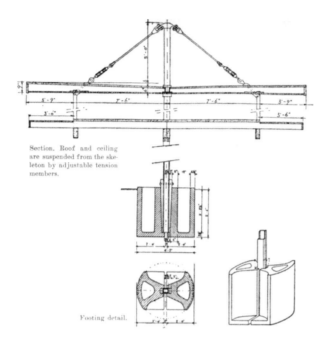

Section. Roof and ceiling are suspended from the skeleton by adjustable tension members.

Footing detail.

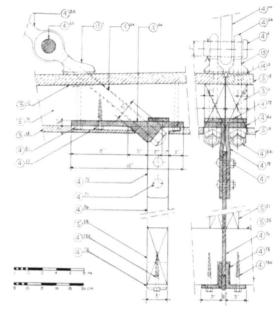

Construction detail.

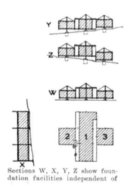

Y

Z

W

X

2 1 3

Sections W, X, Y, Z show foundation facilities independent of

Prefabricated "one plus two" expandable dwellings of Diatom construction.

5.7

Richard Neutra, prefabricated house,
construction details (1926).

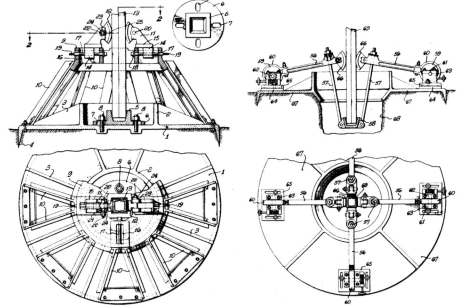

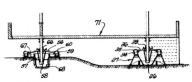

Section

Prefabricated foundation for unrestricted application must be conceived to suit varying conditions of soil and grades.

Example of prefabricated footings.

Neutras two patents of the prefabricated self adjusting foundation.

5.8

Richard Neutra,
prefabricated footings, c. 1923.

motivated by Neutra's lifelong admiration for automobiles and the methods of their production, but also by his interest in factory-based serial manufacture.

ARCHITECTURE EN SÉRIE

For all systems of prefabrication, repetition was essential, and Neutra returned to this point throughout his writings and throughout his career. Repeatability was key, he thought, in design and construction, but it was also essential in financing, rational land use and planning, homeownership, and the mass distribution of valued goods—matters of social and economic organization. As would be expected, the wide application or interpretation of this principle would have repercussions beyond the design of an individual building, for example on the layout of suburban settlements in the United States, which increased in density as a result of continued population growth and the expansion of residential districts into unbuilt or rural areas. The analogy between mechanisms of architectural construction and the automobile industry was commonplace at this time, as is well known; but in Neutra's case the analogy was not principally a matter of appearance or of streamlining, which he often criticized, but of manufacture, use, and reuse. He once confessed his equal respect for Frank Lloyd Wright and Henry Ford. This was a sensible and presumably shared sentiment in the United States in the war years.

Neutra's early design for a prefabricated house was followed by many other projects that incorporated factory-made components. He aspired to design prototypes for wide-ranging industrial application. In a 1946 article published in an issue of *L'Architecture d'Aujourd'hui* devoted to his work—an article that took for granted the possibility of converting the assets of the war industry for use in the housing industry—Neutra used the possibility of repetition as the measure of success in contemporary design: "whatever we design today, the immense number of careful technical details we conceive—all of it has its true contemporary significance only if it does not aim at uniqueness, but at an applicability for repetitive production, for production *en série*."[9] This measure of success was also recognized by Marcel Lods, the president of the French Association of Architect-Prefabricators, for he stressed in the same journal that Neutra fully embraced the machine production of architectural materials, making his designs both contemporary and "classic."[10]

In addition to his own inventions for production "*en série*," Neutra tried to incorporate premade elements designed by others. One instructive example is

Buckminster Fuller's "dymaxion bathroom"—a highly compact and efficient plumbing core—which Neutra installed in a house for John Nicholas Brown, built in New York in 1938. The example is interesting because the installation led Neutra to question the use of all elements of this kind in houses.[11] In *Survival through Design,* Neutra recalled a comment from his client's six-year-old son about the incongruity of his grandmother using this shiny metal die-stamped unit: "imagine grandmother in that bathtub, all made in the shop." Provoked by this memory, he wondered if everyone could or should be accommodated by units such as this; after all, he continued, families and their households were established over generations. How can a house made in the shop stand up to long-term use and be manufactured in a sufficient variety of forms to accommodate a range of preferences that develop over time? How can prefabrications have "personality"? Can standardization allow for choice? For Neutra these were important questions, and ones that were more pressing in the design of a house than in the production of a car. Homes provide a sense of anchorage or rootedness, which is never the purpose of a car. Can the technology of car production, when applied to house construction, allow for the emotional and visual character that connotes the house? Neutra implied that Fuller was insensitive to this problem, or at least hadn't answered this basic question.

While Neutra's writings are not definitive on this issue, his buildings do provide insights into the possible reconciliation between prefabrication and what he saw as human needs. A case in point is his own house and office, which he named the VDL House in honor of C. H. van der Leeuw, the industrialist who financed the van Nelle tobacco factory and whose financing allowed Neutra to build the house. Neutra had met van der Leeuw in Zurich and visited him in his Rotterdam house (a house that experimented with many of the devices Neutra introduced into his Health and VDL houses). After these early contacts, Neutra and van der Leeuw established a working friendship. One day in 1923, Neutra reported, "[van der Leeuw] pulled out a checkbook and asked, 'How much do you need?'"[12] This support and their friendship depended partly on their shared dedication to modern architecture but also on their mutual interest in matters of health and psychological well-being. The construction of the VDL House, however, was actually paid for with funds or donations from three sources: van der Leeuw, Neutra himself, and local building material suppliers whose donated products Neutra obtained with the promise that the building's likely importance would bring their products favorable publicity.

The structural system of the VDL House is hybrid: unlike his earlier and already very famous Health House (the Lovell house of 1929), which has a structural frame built out of steel, this building's load-bearing system was built out of wood, much like a traditional balloon frame but not entirely so because of the greater interval between the studs (thirty-nine and a half inches rather than sixteen inches) and the dimension of the studs themselves, which were made about double their typical size.[13] This altered dimensioning allowed for the long horizontal windows Neutra desired. It also required fewer experiments on the builder's part, which lowered the cost of the construction. The balloon frame and references to past construction systems are hidden, however, for there is nothing "traditional" about the building's appearance; its load-bearing timber "chassis" was completely covered by a layer of stucco and then finished with a coat of aluminum paint, giving it a modern and machined appearance. The paint also covers both wood and sheet-metal trim. Although this uniform surface treatment conceals the range of materials used in the building, one cannot say it dematerializes the building, for the result and the aim, it seems, are a very specific material quality, that of being metallic. However, the building appears metallic only in color, brightness, and flatness, because the sort of connections that typify sheet-metal fabrication were unnecessary with stucco and therefore are nowhere apparent. While modern materials and methods were, indeed, used on the inside of this building, the outside is more an image of an industrialized building than one in fact.

The same is not true of Neutra's work in the next few years, however. If the VDL House gave him an image of what a modern building should look like, the Beard house, begun in 1934, demonstrated one way that it could be built. It is important to stress that Neutra's use of industrialized materials was atypical and unconventional. In place of either wood or steel structural columns, Neutra used rolled sections of corrugated steel to support the roof of the Beard house. His use of this material was unconventional, even subversive, for it is normally used for decking and covered with concrete. Yet in this house it was used vertically, with the bottom embedded in a concrete footing (allowing the sheets of steel to act rather like a vertical cantilever) while the top was welded to the bar joists that support the plane of the roof. The inside surface of this vertical "decking" was lined with plaster, its outer side with vertical panels of sheet steel—again covered with aluminum paint. In addition to its structural economy, this system had the merit of allowing for an effective and ingenious system of thermal control: air

5.9

Richard Neutra, VDL House,
Silverlake, California, 1933.

5.10
Richard Neutra, Beard house,
under construction,
Altadena, California, 1935.

intakes at the base of the exterior walls and vents at the top provide a convection or "stack effect" of warm air during summer months through "vertical flues" (thus cooling the building), while the cavities beneath the linoleum and concrete floor allow heated air to warm the rooms above through radiant heating.

The Beard house won the 1934 Gold Medal Award in the Better Homes in America Competition. The competition jury, which included George Howe and Joseph Hudnut, praised the design as a "serious study in which structure and mechanical equipment admirably express the space composition as a satisfactory environment for a given set of living conditions . . . and an effort to solve the problem of American life in a given locality and under given conditions."[14] This expresses very well Neutra's sense of the opportunities and difficulties of building with industrialized elements: the need to build for modern patterns of life and to respond to given circumstances of site and climate.

Three issues are intertwined in this problem: manufacturing practices, contemporary dwelling habits, and the qualities of the site or region in which the building is located. One of Neutra's most sustained treatments of this problem began with the development of his thoughts on repetition in building manufacture. He claimed to have been very impressed in his youth by Adolf Loos's deep respect for well-crafted artifacts: Cremona violins, Viennese cabinet work (before Victorianism and art nouveau stylizing), and American woodwork—even the oak toilet seat. All of these artifacts were produced repetitively. Neutra, however, extended Loos's praise for type objects, such as the Thonet chair, to broad support for repetitive production as such: "perhaps this strangely sparked my admiration for the United States' precise though repetitive industrialized technology."[15] What Loos found in chairs made by his favorite craftsman, Josef Veillich, Neutra found in anonymously produced doorknobs, appliances, tools, and toilet seats. This observation allowed him to overcome or at least to neglect the differences between craft and machine production, differences that many architects in the preceding decades had carefully observed and hotly debated. And he went further. Turning to the second issue involved in the problem of repetition, that of dwelling needs, Neutra associated mass-produced objects with the "organic common denominator(s) of the species." While he didn't cite Le Corbusier in developing his argument, his claims seem very similar to those concerning "human limb objects" and the "law of mechanical selection" put forward in *L'art décoratif d'aujourd'hui* of 1925 (two years after Neutra had settled in America). Neutra thought that American industry, unimpeded by the interests of "petty tradespeople, who had lost their traditional touch with human beings," could attend to the needs and opportunities of contemporary living. This had been done in the mass production of furnishings and could also be done in the serial production of strictly architectural elements: cladding systems, fenestration, flooring materials, lighting equipment, and so on.

The third issue, that of site or region, concerned the use of new materials, which were not only repetitively produced but also "biologically" determined to suit contemporary lifestyles. These materials would also contextualize designs and give groupings of buildings and entire regions character and identity. Writing about the windows of his famous Health House, for example, Neutra observed: "through continuity of fenestration, [and] linkage with the landscape, we should draw again on what the vitally dynamic natural scene had been for a hundred thousand years . . . a human habitat."[16] Mass production and site specificity are not contradictory. "Regional uniformity in planning the vast uniformity of human dwellings existed all over the globe . . . the appearance of [preindustrial villages throughout the world] is most often one of natural uniformity . . . modes of fenestration, sash, door, and wall construction within one locality are almost exactly the same all the way through . . . a standard."[17] This is what he had seen in the Taos pueblos used to conclude *Wie baut Amerika*. The same kind of standard could be achieved, he thought, with factory-made elements. To calm those who might suspect the likelihood of monotony in such a prospect, Neutra reported that no settlement in Japan is tedious, despite the high degree of architectural uniformity in each region: Kyoto is not boring. He assumed that the same uniformity could be produced in modern America. In an interesting twist in his argument, Neutra observed that modern industry, in its early phase, did not lead to uniformity but to its opposite, spurious variety, because it sustained so many choices. But the outcome of industrialization and of repetition could be different. "Lost unity," he said, must be restored: "can it possibly be done now on another basis than that of machine production?"[18]

The answer to this question and the arguments that support it can be brought out in full force by considering one additional element from Neutra's work. From the middle part of his career, Neutra became famous for his "open air" school designs. Although his first project of this type appeared in *Wie baut Amerika,* he was particularly active in developing it in the 1930s and 1940s. In virtually all of his designs, the classroom had several characteristic features: clerestory glazing on the corridor side, movable furnishings within the room, a

5.11

Richard Neutra,

Emerson Junior High School,

classroom and patio, Los Angeles, 1938.

window wall on the garden or yard side, adjustable awnings also on this side to control solar gain and glare, and—the most significant element—a sliding glass partition wall/door that allowed for teaching to occur both inside and out. Several photographs and drawings in his publications illustrate this, often with children sitting in an arc that originates at the blackboard, passes from inside to outside, and terminates at the base of a tree, which substitutes its leafy canopy for the building's trabeated ceiling in providing a sense of enclosure. The desire was for spatial expansion or "openness," which was proposed as the setting for modern patterns of education, patterns in which the teacher became "a member of an active group who works freely around the classroom."[19] This design was also proposed as a prototype that would be suitable for serial production. Once again, repetition was thought to be key, and it was to be found in type form, construction elements, functional needs, and siting techniques. Repetition so conceived and realized was to lead to the "unity" that Neutra admired in preindustrial culture—Taos or Kyoto—and saw as the promise of modern standardization. The child and the desk; the window, sliding door, structural frame, and cladding panels; the rooms, buildings, and site layouts were all conceived *en série,* making out of so many individual elements a unified whole.

The kind of uniformity Neutra observed in ancient villages was never fully realized in his buildings—nor could it be in an age that was fast becoming industrialized. At the same time, he never realized the kind of uniformity proposed in the "mass-produced" buildings of individuals like Buckminster Fuller, for the age was not yet entirely industrialized. Perhaps it will be clearer to say that the industrialization of buildings was a project, not (yet) a condition. Both of these alternate images of complete unity are utopian, the first regressive, the second progressive. As a matter of built fact, Neutra's "industrialized" or "serialized" constructions exist somewhere between these two extremes: mass-produced elements are used, and used in series, but they are always integrated into elements that are unique to each design, like the "vertical cantilever" in the Beard house. This middle position makes the projects both conceptually and technically imperfect—imperfectly standardized—but it also gives them a sense of concreteness that the nostalgic and futuristic examples lack. The same style of thinking is apparent in Neutra's distance from Loos's appeal to traditional craft and in his unease with Fuller's dymaxion tub. Because vernacular construction was a lost unity and industrialized assembly had not yet been achieved, the kind of building that Neutra's work illustrates should be described with terms other than those of craft construction or standardized assembly—perhaps with the term we have used to characterize the juxtaposition of elements in Albert Kahn's and Mies's work: assemblage. But for Neutra, the assemblage was not one of building masses (front and back), as it had been for Kahn, but of all those elements that were attached to one another in his construction details, in their most precise resolution. The play or tolerance between site-specific (wet) and mass-produced (dry) elements is decisive in these details. Because moldings were eliminated, the play between old and new materials was "marked" by negative details or by plastic sealants, concealing or covering the lines of differential movement. While these connections were the location of Neutra's most inventive solutions, they were also the places of performance failure, testifying to the difficulty of this middle position. His use of aluminum paint to cover cladding panels, wood trim, and steel panels indicates the same approach to integrating industrial and preindustrial materials and methods. Because its use recognizes material difference (while trying to hide it) and tries to approximate sameness (of color and "finish"), it can be seen as both an instrument and symbol of unity, one that heightens the qualities of some elements while hiding those of others. Paint allowed Neutra to get close to perfect uniformity, thereby building in the manner of both past and future America, in appearance at least.

FABRICATION PROCESSES

The "concreteness" of Neutra's buildings is what Marcel Lods, the great proponent of standardization in France, enthusiastically praised. In claiming that Neutra was both contemporary and classic, Lods explained that Neutra had acted in his time the way the "classics" had in theirs, that is, answering the needs of an epoch by using "to a maximum extent the material means it has to offer." An example of this, Lods thought, was the use of the "immense sliding glass partitions which alternately created a perfectly closed room, or an open hall extending itself into the garden . . . through which nature could enter the house [or school]."[20] Writing this in 1946, Lods could equally well have been describing the walls of the *Ecole en plein air* in Suresnes that he had designed and built together with Eugène Beaudouin in 1935, the same year as Neutra's Los Angeles school project. The Suresnes school also has classrooms enclosed by movable walls, but here on three sides rather than one; they fold in on themselves like internal shutters rather than swinging out like a door, and consist of multiple glass panes of

5.12
Eugène Beaudouin and Marcel Lods,
Open-Air School, Suresnes, France,
1935.

traditional dimension rather than an "immense" sheet of glass.[21] This last difference is indicative of the basic differences between prefabrication in France and America at this time.

The construction system used by Beaudouin and Lods was one they had developed two years earlier in their work for the small city of Dracy. Although their later work at Clichy, in collaboration with Jean Prouvé, utilized different materials, it too emerged out of the same approach to prefabrication, in which three sorts of materials or elements were integrated: (1) traditional "wet" methods and preindustrial materials, (2) modern mass-produced elements available to all architects for all sorts of projects, and (3) prefabricated elements designed for this or very similar projects. Certainly other architects and builders had designed elements to be produced repetitively, but in the work of Beaudouin and Lods these elements take on a much more important and pervasive role.

The construction system of the open-air school at Suresnes consists of standardized parts for both walls and floors, which are supported on a steel frame. Steel is not used throughout for load-bearing, however, for the concrete slabs of the floor rest on precast reinforced concrete T section beams, which are in turn supported by the steel frame. The deep section created by these beams allows for the placement of heating elements: ducts through which warm air is passed and then vented through grates placed around the perimeter of the room, and steel tubes through which steam is circulated, heating the entire floor surface above.

The heterogeneous character of the building's structural frame is also apparent in its relationship to the cladding system: the frame is immured in the walls on the north side and exposed on the walls that face the south. This contrast is a function of siting and orientation: to the north, noise from traffic and distracting views are excluded by thick walls made of masonry infill construction, clad on the outside with standardized precast concrete panels; whereas to the south, where views can open onto a landscape and natural daylight can be used to illuminate the interiors, thin walls of lightweight metal cladding and glazing have been used. The first walling system contains the frame while the second exposes it, contrasting what might be called laminated and delaminated walls. Without describing the construction system further, it is apparent that this building is elaborately composite, both of materials and of types of components. It would be wrong, however, to say that it is expressively or pictorially so, for the variations arose from rather practical considerations, matters of performance, with respect to the use of the building, its site, and concerns of heating or making a sensible response to the climate. These were the same kinds of considerations that led Neutra to develop "imperfect" or "nearly uniform" systems of construction and assembly—assemblage—in view of his details especially. And he, too, integrated laminated and delaminated cladding systems in individual buildings. Where Beaudouin and Lods differ is in their use of more standardized elements *of their own design.* The whole of the north facade, for example, is clad in precast concrete panels, finished with pebbles embedded in their surface.

The approach taken in the French case emphasized and required great attention to the *process* of building. Lods is well known for having concerned himself with this chiefly. Throughout his career he visited construction sites and photographically documented the different phases or steps of the building's development. From the documentary point of view, no one of these steps was more important than any of the others, not even the last, when the building was ready for occupation, for that stage was to be followed by others in the lifetime of the building, when exigencies of use or external factors would call for modifications to its physical fabric. These, too, were seen as part of its "constructed" reality, *essentially so.* Lods's documentary work testifies to his preoccupation with the temporal unfolding of a built work, during which elements with different origins (on the site, in the fabricator's shop, or from the factory) were integrated together. Lods's sense of the building's image or appearance resulted from the "facts" of its construction. To put this point more strongly, his attention to the process of building led him to "devisualize" architecture or at least to indefinitely postpone the identification of a final image, recognizing that each image that appears "now" will be followed by another "then."

If the school at Suresnes illustrates the architectural consequences of this kind of delay, by revealing the integration of various technologies it sustains, later buildings by Lods and Beaudouin also testify to the importance of a *constructeur* in the whole process, especially a *constructeur* such as Jean Prouvé, whose work in design and manufacture anticipated on-site adjustments and the integration of different sorts of elements.

"FOR MANY YEARS I WORE THE LEATHER APRON"

Design and manufacture merge in Jean Prouvé's work, and do so in ways that were largely unprecedented in architecture. From the time of his early training in Nancy through his apprenticeships in the metal trades and the establishment of his own "workshops," Prouvé was a designer who had little patience for the graphic (or pictorial) media of design, preferring instead to transform his sketches into full-scale models with few intermediate steps: "I believe you have to build a preliminary version the moment you think of it, test it out, make corrections, get opinions on it, and only then, if it is worthwhile, do you settle all the details in very precise drawings."[22] Because of his training in metal workshops, he was entirely able to build his designs, as well as models of his designs, himself. His collaborators were able to do so too. In his workshop, Prouvé established what has been called "worker participation," which meant that collaborators had neither management nor a "designer" above them to give them instructions and determine their work. It also meant that those who participated in the development of the project shared in the rewards it received, whether financial or professional. The hierarchical system taken for granted in Fordism, or its architectural equivalent in Albert Kahn's office, had no place in Prouvé's shop. Individuals with similar training and equivalent responsibility worked together to build what they designed. And they designed prototypes—for furniture, structural framing, and architectural cladding, especially.

Many of the architectural elements that came out of the Prouvé workshops are structural hybrids, in which frame cannot be separated from skin. Prouvé was very inventive with cladding, in which he was the first to use folded sheet metal for architectural construction. Like others of the time, he was inspired by aircraft engineering and technology, and more than others he demonstrated how its techniques could be used in building construction. This was particularly apparent in his design and manufacture of cladding elements.

In some of Prouvé's work, cladding panels were "commensurate" with the building's structure, thus expressing its intervals. Dimensional coordination of this kind assumed the existence of a module as an element of both prefabrication and of measure. The panels on the Buc Pavilion at the Roland Garros Flying Club, for example, conform to a module and dimensional interval derived from the spacing or gaps between the vertical posts.[23] In this instance, the frame is not concealed, as it was in later buildings; its measures are re-represented by the cladding module. This attitude toward the frame changed in other buildings, such as the Maison du Peuple, where the load-bearing posts are far less significant. The difference is not just that they are no longer visible in some of the building's parts, nor that the spacing between them sets the dimension of the module; instead, the overall appearance of the building now results from the qualities of the wall

5.13
Eugène Beaudouin, Marcel Lods,
Vladimir Bodiansky, and Jean Prouvé,
Maison du Peuple, market hall, Clichy,
France, 1939.

panels themselves, and these qualities result largely from the exigencies of industrialized production. It is for this reason that the Maison du Peuple is so revolutionary. Rather than referring to visual qualities of its site, to traditional proportional systems, or to former and preindustrial modes of construction, this exterior enclosure—which is hard to call a facade—testifies to its origins in a workshop and development in factory production. If this building has an "image," even an "image of," then production is what appears. This is similar to what we have seen in Kahn's factory buildings, but there are important differences between the two examples. The conditions of the panel's workshop origin in Prouvé's example are as new as they are specific: panels were designed for the optimization of building production. For purposes of construction, the panels were to be transportable, self-supporting, and easily assembled. Yet, quite apart from evidence of its serial production, the panel contains in its form the signature of Prouvé's hand; it was his design, and this, too, is revolutionary, if not in kind then in degree. This could be called standardization by design, something many architects have dreamed of but few have had the skills to accomplish. Prouvé's signature gives the panel, and by extension the building, its particularity. Because any number of panels are expected to result from optimized production and to sustain efficient assembly on a building site, choice of one over another (on the market) results from the recognition and selection of such a "signature," generally most apparent in its profile.

These panels give the building its identity by simultaneously acting as wall and facade. Kahn never intended this, and neither Howe and Lescaze nor Neutra could have accomplished it, because their buildings were only partly standardized. Panels such as these accomplish yet another purpose of walling: they give to the exterior enclosure self-supporting tectonic integrity. In the Maison du Peuple, the panels, measuring one by four meters, clip together at their base and top and are tied back to the top side of the building's slabs with metal angles. Neither the columns nor the slabs *support* the walls. Interlocked as a three-dimensional enclosure, the panels resemble the self-supporting body and unitary construction of the well-know Citroën "Traction-avant" of 1934.[24] The same is true in Prouvé's Unesco building; the columns bear the load of the slabs but leave the panels free to support themselves.

To the degree that cladding systems such as this totalize enclosure or containment, the design of buildings closely approximates that of airplanes and automobiles, especially of airplanes. Furthermore, the "construction" of buildings approximates even more closely the ideal of assembly. Yet when the design and manufacture of architectural elements seem to assimilate themselves most closely to aircraft and automobile production, a significant difference asserts itself: Prouvé's profiles marked his buildings with his own interpretation of the problem at hand. And in the graphic and manual reasoning of that interpretation, the uniqueness of the project preserved its place.

Still, the question concerning "uniqueness" is not fully answered by this observation, for the individuality that resulted from this process of design, manufacture, and construction did not necessarily lead to the singularity of individual buildings, only to those of a kind. That Prouvé was aware of this can be seen in his comments on variety within serial construction, comments that arose in consideration of the organization of the modern building process.

Prouvé firmly stated that the designer who keeps himself distant from the demands of industrial construction should not be called an architect. At the same time, the builders of aircraft, dams, and similar constructions could, he thought, properly be called "architects." Discussing the overall organization of the building process, he observed that the architect who is "not integrated into industry" will be left behind modern times. So, too, for buildings; their relevance derives from their incorporation of industrial methods. Thus, the systematic unity of parts that characterized machine production of all kinds was to be found in buildings, too. Prouvé wrote: "I cannot agree in any way to . . . open-system prefabrication. This can only be of use for the insertion of individual elements into integrated designs and to introduce an element of *variety*. . . . Let us therefore make a start with closed systems—a sounder conception as I see it."[25] In advocating "closed systems," Prouvé had in mind the fact that machines were seldom assembled from components of different origins. Were it to follow this model, architecture too, particularly that of houses, would be conceived and realized as a closed system. In such a system, the engineer would no longer supply the (compositionally skilled) architect with elements to be inserted into designs when and wherever necessary, but would work in collaboration with the architect, collaborating so closely that they would effectively become one (an idea that explains Prouvé's praise for individuals like Perret and Nervi). Even better—best—would be for the architect to be an engineer. The individuality or identity of the project would then arise out of what Prouvé called its constructional conception.

OPEN AND CLOSED SYSTEMS OF CONSTRUCTION

In the postwar period, workshop processes like Jean Prouvé's were not the only basis for developing a building's identity or uniqueness, despite the premises and practices of repetitive production. We have observed that Prouvé's was, in fact, a rather isolated case, even though many architects argued for what he actually practiced. For others who built in the postwar years, "open systems" were not to be rejected, as he had argued, but accepted and developed, as is evident in the work of Neutra and Lods. The same is true for architects working in other countries, where the open process was seen to be more realistic—and this realism had both a pragmatic and an ethical dimension, given the range of pressures on postwar housing needs. These architects utilized elements with different origins (factory and craft origins), while they attempted to achieve the rationality and coherence of organization that characterized Prouvé's work. Modern manufacturing standards were accepted, but modified.

Already in the 1950s the younger generation of CIAM supporters who formed Team 10 introduced a range of materials in their buildings in reaction to what they saw as the "contemporary" version of modernism, a version that demonstrated the misuse of traditional motifs and materials. This reaction came to be called "New Brutalism." But new ways of using materials was not all that characterized brutalist buildings; also important was the reevaluation of the advanced buildings of the 1920s and 1930s, the lessons of which, according to Reyner Banham, had been forgotten. Similarly significant was the use of proportions in design, then popularly described by Rudolf Wittkower.[1] The preoccupation with a range of materials and their various uses was further strengthened by renewed contact with Japanese precedents—not as examples of the craft tradition, much appreciated by Frank Lloyd Wright, nor as an indication of the essential role of structure and screen, as they were for Mies, but as objects of what Banham called an "intellectual appraisal."

The work of Alison and Peter Smithson at Hunstanton exhibits little of the idealization of construction that typified Prouvé's buildings or those of Mies van der Rohe, whose work in both Germany and the United States was nevertheless very important to them. Rather than correcting the external appearance of the building's structure, as Mies had done at his Lake Shore Drive apartments, the Smithsons wanted their building to present the "facts" of construction more directly, unadorned; not "as if" they were something they weren't, but as they were themselves. Thus their work exemplifies the "realism" we have mentioned. A comparison of two details—the corner column at Mies's Memorial Hall, Illinois Institute of Technology, and the corner column at the Smithsons' Hunstanton School—indicates the differences between the two approaches. In the IIT building the columns are recessed from the planes of the exterior walls, creating a spatial void that gives the effect of an absent or missing column. Further, the construction of the column is composite, partly column and partly wall: standard sections are welded together for the combined purpose of supporting and articulating the corner. On the inside of the building, this results in the separation of the column from the walls. Once separated, their relationship needed to be reconsidered or negotiated in each case, depending on the various circumstances within the building. At Hunstanton, by contrast, the corner column is coplanar with the exterior walls. Because the steel sections that separate the building's lower and upper floor are coplanar with the column, however, the column's supporting role is deemphasized, making it akin to the border of a picture frame. This also means the distinction between column and cladding is reduced; as the columns join the horizontal elements in the construction of an atectonic frame or border, they take on the appearance of surface. Yet, despite its atectonic planarity, this border's color distinguishes it from the walling. Brick panels contrast with it, as do glazed surfaces. With the introduction of these two materials came others, all appearing as "facts" of construction. The use of such a range of material facts, understood to be expressive in their own right, distinguishes this building from those of Mies and Prouvé. It also illustrates why the work of the Smithsons shows a different approach to the idea of the "system"—

6.1

Alison and Peter Smithson,
Hunstanton School, Norfolk, England,
1954. © John T. Hansell.

not closed but open, yet still dependent on the facts of building for its identity and image.

BRUTAL FACTS OF BUILDING

At Hunstanton the glazing system is one of the building's most significant achievements and greatest failures. The aim and the problem involved the assembly of contemporary materials in connections that did not rely on covering or mediating elements. The glass was fixed directly into a steel channel, which in turn was directly welded to the main structural frame. This detail eliminated the necessity of subframes, but at the same time required greater accuracy in tolerances. Differential thermal expansion led to flexing and cracking of the glass, a problem that was eventually solved by the introduction of wooden subframes. These alterations denied the intended purity of the solution, a purity that was originally also apparent in the interiors (and is still visible there), especially in the exposed electrical and plumbing services. Perhaps it is extreme to call this kind of directness or exposure "brutal," but that term does indicate the desire to let the elements themselves give the building its expression. Banham suggested that this was, for the Smithsons, not an aesthetic but an ethical concern, meaning that the toleration of heterogeneous solutions (and the rejection of early modernist idealism) indicated sensitivity to the social and economic needs of the time.

Other examples from the same period indicate a similar interest in the "brutal" facts of building: Louis I. Kahn's Yale University Art Gallery (especially the "impress" of shuttering on the concrete wall that enclosed its main staircase), or the Free University Arts Building in Berlin by Candilis, Josic and Woods (particularly the Cor Ten steel, the color of which Peter Smithson compared to a used penny). In these examples and others, the process of building is rationalized. Also, some of the elements are industrialized, but not all of them. The image or expression of the building is hybrid, the result of combining modern with traditional materials, such as brick; and some modern materials, such as Cor Ten steel, assume the qualities of traditional ones. Whether aluminum and glass, or *béton brut* and brick, the materials themselves had become as important as the rationality of the building process.

The call for attention to materials themselves and for an architecture of the art of building had been made before. Perhaps this call was put forth most

6.2
Louis I. Kahn,
Yale University Art Gallery,
New Haven, 1953.

6.3
Candilis, Josic and Woods
with Jean Prouvé, Arts Building,
Free University, Berlin, 1973.

persuasively or stridently by Hannes Meyer.[2] In the case of brutalism, however, the acceptance of "traditional" materials, and for Kahn the preoccupation with "archaic" themes, led to an architecture of material texture. The "facts of construction" were also important in contemporary artwork. Eduardo Paolozzi, a friend and collaborator of the Smithsons in the Independent Group, was at this time utilizing *impasto* technique in his artwork. The interest in material surface in these examples—constructions using *béton brut,* Cor Ten, brick, or *impasto*—brought about a qualification or adjustment to the basic premises of modernism: the standards of contemporary industry were to be reconciled with earlier types of material and methods of construction. In this way, the reality of older methods was brought into the present. This pragmatic, less iconic modernism did not attempt to disguise the difficulty of its realization, nor did it exclude the darker aspects of the parallel between life and art.

FACTS OF BUILDING AND OF LIFE

James Stirling, in his comments on Le Corbusier's Maisons Jaoul (1952–1957), observed that nothing of this building's technology was unavailable to medieval builders.[3] Even if extreme, this statement testifies to his sense, and presumably other architects', that the master had reevaluated the role of modern methods and materials in postwar building. The construction of the paired houses in Paris resulted from the labors of Algerian workmen. Despite Stirling's remark about their lack of technological innovation, the Maisons Jaoul seem to have inspired the Ham Common apartments he designed in collaboration with James Gowan (1955–1958). Reyner Banham observed that the use of these everyday materials did not arise out of philosophical sympathy alone but also because of the "grinding economic necessity that made any but the most banal materials unthinkable for smaller house building."[4] If the spatial complexity of the Maisons Jaoul caused the builders to construct joints of less precision, the repetitive forms of the Ham Common apartments allowed for sharper distinctions between the building's different materials. Negative joints also contribute to the impression of distinct surfaces or material textures juxtaposed against one another; the result seems less spontaneous than Jaoul but more refined, formal, and elemental. For this reason, it might seem wise to exclude the Ham Common building from the canon of brutalist works. Nevertheless, if the walls of the Parisian example have great

6.4
Marcel Breuer with Hamilton Smith
and Robert F. Gatje Associates,
University Heights,
New York University, New York,
1956–1961.

6.5
Le Corbusier,
Maisons Jaoul, Paris, 1957.

6.6
James Stirling and James Gowan,
Ham Common apartments,
London, 1958.

depth, those of the English apartments restate the importance of surface planarity, despite the "thickness" associated with the use of brick.

This change of interests did not arise out of matters of building production alone, for interconnected with this construction technique were cultural conditions. While the postwar period in England was certainly a time of pressing need, it was not one of great wealth. At the same time, the existing city was not without iconic potential, even in its poorer sections. Members of the Independent Group, such as Nigel Henderson, saw urban areas like Bethnal Green as laboratories for investigations into "neighborhood anthropology" and the "tribal liaisons" of the city's back streets and less-affluent quarters. But to see studies resulting from this anthropology as indications of social realism is to distort or neglect its contact with avant-garde art, particularly that of French origin (Brassaï, Giacometti, Cartier-Bresson, etc.) but also American developments such as the photographs of Walker Evans. The "Patio and Pavilion" collaboration of Nigel Henderson, Eduardo Paolozzi, and the Smithsons for the "This Is Tomorrow" exhibition of 1956 illustrated not only chunks or bits of Englishness in collage— English oak, for example—but also evidence of the aftermath of the war: wandering children, charred wood, rusted bicycle wheels. Again, the aim was not documentary realism, although that was partly the result, but an aesthetic transformation of the condition. Henderson, for example, was fascinated by the spectral and fragmented images of shop windows. In a photograph of such a scene, one can see not only the goods on display but also, by virtue of a carefully chosen point of view and darkroom techniques, much more besides: figures passing by, aspects of the adjoining buildings and streets, traces of the shop interior, and qualities of the glass itself. Montage techniques were used in the production of images like this, as were the methods of surrealism, particularly chance encounter. Perhaps nothing could be further from the idea of a closed system. Like the "Patio and Pavilion" materials, the contents of the "Grille" presented by the Smithsons at the 1953 CIAM 9 conference were meant to integrate the variety and diversity of human association in contemporary life, despite the clarity of its organizational framework.

If architectural design is to work with "found" materials, and to do so without prejudice to either traditional or modern ones, if it is to accept all materials that are available within the limits of a given social, economic, and cultural condition, then construction will define itself as a struggle to integrate and to reconcile materials of different origins. Just as modern and traditional materials must

6.7
Nigel Henderson,
Newsagent, East London, 1952.

enter into new and unforeseen relationships, so must the processes by which they are made: site work must coordinate hand- and machine-made elements. Alison and Peter Smithson, in "The 'As Found' and the 'Found,'" related this task to the one performed by a number of twentieth-century artists, particularly Dubuffet, Pollock, and Duchamp.[5] The Smithsons' emphasis on process directed attention to how a work is produced: "as the stock of made-objects [some of which could be factory-made] is continuously renewed by the activities arising from different needs, intelligences, and sensibilities of each period, the art activity of wit-and-eye founded on these objects can continue."

A parallel approach can be seen in Colin Rowe and Fred Koetter's later *Collage City* (1978). Citing Lévi-Strauss, Rowe and Koetter envisaged a middle position for the artist/architect, somewhere between the "odd job man" and the scientist, for these two are not only distinct but reciprocal: "the scientist and the *bricoleur* are to be distinguished 'by the inverse functions which they assign to event and structures as means and ends, the scientist creating events . . . by means of structures and the *bricoleur* creating structures by means of events.'"[6] Lévi-Strauss characterized the productive activities of the *bricoleur* as dependent on materials and techniques that were immediately available. Rowe and Koetter described this as an acceptance of "what is at hand." Their sense of the "available" is similar to what we have seen in the brutalist sense of the concrete "facts" of a situation. In Ham Common Stirling and Gowan assembled both the building's "functional" elements and the materials of its construction. This attention to the building's program of uses cannot be identified with old-style functionalism, however, nor with the closed-system style of thinking that it assumed. The vocabulary of collage and "oddments" indicates that there is in this example a kind of openness that severs the causal link between function and form. This could be called an aesthetic of functionalism, but such an account would be partial, for the inventive, even devious distribution of functional elements rested upon an unconventional interpretation of the building's program. Thus, both pragmatic and aesthetic interests were operative in this case; the juxtaposition of volumes presumed both programmatic invention and the use of images, some of which seem to have been derived from the projects of Konstantin Melnikov, Frank Lloyd Wright, and Theo van Doesburg.

Yet the practice of working with what is "at hand" need not appropriate images, as is suggested by a passage from Lévi-Strauss that Rowe and Koetter didn't cite. In *The Savage Mind,* the anthropologist defined his sense of "bricolage" as follows: "the bricoleur 'speaks' not only *with* things . . . but also through the medium of things: as giving an account of his personality and life by the choice he makes between the limited possibilities."[7]

INVENTION AND LIMITED MEANS

From our point of view, an architect who exemplifies this manner of "working through things" with "limited means" better than most of the time is Alejandro de la Sota, who practiced in Spain during this same period. While clearly acknowledging the significant contribution of the "masters"—Wright, Le Corbusier, Mies—de la Sota took an approach that was deliberately less singular and polemical; his projects appear more empirical and pragmatic than ideological. As such, his approach was not unlike that of the Team 10 members—of the Smithsons certainly, but also of José Antonio Coderch, a friend of de la Sota. For the Team 10 group, the war resulted in the need for an architecture of austerity, in which limited means would be the best way to achieve relevant solutions. De la Sota's commitment to what he termed architectural "simplicity" was wholly in keeping with this aim, but, as with the most interesting of the Team 10 projects, his solutions were invariably dependent on the transgression of those very limits, whether material or technical.

De la Sota's own version of this condition is best illustrated by his recollection of a chance encounter with Le Corbusier in the 1950s, during the construction of the Unité d'Habitation in Berlin. He was struck by Le Corbusier's renunciation of the German builders' constant drive toward perfection: "It looked as if they [the builders] had passed their tongues over the concrete before letting it set," he recalls Le Corbusier saying.[8] For de la Sota, who was used to the less-than-perfect standards of construction in Spain after the war, Le Corbusier's call for an architecture of "imperfection" provided a crucial inspiration; in fact, his quest for imperfection gave his work its "elegance." Equally, imperfection resisted the ideality of the image, then as now assumed by some to be the a priori task of architecture.

In the Arvesú house, built in Madrid in 1955, de la Sota developed an inward-looking architecture that "turned its back on the world," partly in response to the conditions of the site. The architect claimed that if it had been left to him he would not have placed a single window on the street facade; in fact, a compromise with the client resulted in a few small openings. Regardless,

6.8
José Antonio Coderch,
apartment house, La Barceloneta,
Spain, 1954.

the rough undulating brick walls of the facade constitute a mass reminiscent of baroque architecture, the silence of which is heightened by the modulations of sunlight on its uneven surfaces. The building demonstrates the value of reticence, as well as de la Sota's mistrust of "representation" as the prioritization of the visual. His denial of the need for architecture to act as the conveyor of messages allowed him to turn the building's back to the world, as if construction facts were not only sufficient but essential.

While completing the Arvesú house, de la Sota was also involved in the construction of the Civil Government building in Tarragona (1956–1961), a project he had won in competition. In a project as public as this one, the problem of representation could not be neglected. In other words, in this instance he came face to face with one of the main dilemmas of the period, to which we have referred earlier: how to achieve monumentality within the "project" of modern architecture. The need for a new monumentality, as articulated by Sigfried Giedion among others, concerned modern architecture's response to the role of public or symbolic buildings, as distinct from the architecture of housing, in which appearance was supposedly derived purely from the consideration of rational necessities.

The Civil Government building in Tarragona had to represent the central government of its province. In de la Sota's initial sketches, the building's civic and residential functions were separated into horizontal and vertical blocks, with a garden in between. The final design combines these uses into a single block, while adding a secondary group of residences on the ground floor. Though the side elevations have many windows, de la Sota kept the main elevation primarily opaque, as he did in the Arvesú house. In this case, however, he worked with the symmetry and asymmetry of deep recesses to create an overall tension and balance, giving the impression of a crack or fault line in the mass of the marble, which in turn reveals the dark surfaces of glass and metal set back from the outer limit of the building.

This formal "imperfection" was achieved through the shifting of the two middle openings to the left and right of the facade's central axis. The openings still share an edge, however—a line in the building's depth that appears as a single point on the facade, a "weak" joint that both denies the structural logic of the facade's visuality and creates its point of balance. De la Sota also juxtaposed different materials—marble, glass, metal—to set up associations from which metonymic descriptions could stem. The building discloses and suggests a form

6.9
Alejandro de la Sota,
Civil Government building,
Tarragona, 1961.

6.10
Alejandro de la Sota,
Civil Government building,
detail, Tarragona, 1961.

of reality that cannot be explained but only described. If monumental and representational, it is not in a "this means that" way.

The Maravillas Gymnasium (1960–1962), probably the most significant demonstration of de la Sota's ideas, is an architecture born out of the resolution and adjustment of all the necessities of the project, including an awkward site and limited financial and material resources. But constraints were the means of invention: "there was little time to worry about a specific architecture, which is why the building does not have any architecture at all . . . or perhaps that is an architecture in itself."[9] As such, this project exemplifies de la Sota's notions of a "logical architecture," by which he meant studying all the far-ranging implications of a project before developing possible ways of resolving its puzzle, making representation an outcome of the design process, not its initial impulse. In this manner of working, the relation between materials and results was of great importance.

De la Sota's constant reference to materials was part of his more general belief in the need for new techniques. In fact, he believed that the transformation of existing technologies, and the inventive use of materials, was actually what produced the *architecture* of his projects. In its reliance on materials and new techniques of their use, de la Sota's method bore some resemblance to art practices of the early part of the twentieth century, particularly those of certain constructivist artists. Here too he paralleled what we have seen in the architecture of the Team 10 group. Yet de la Sota's method of working was more akin to Tatlin's assemblages, for example, than to Picasso's collages. The former rely on the possibilities of materials and their juxtaposition to invent the form of the objects, while the latter recall images of existing objects of everyday use—a chair, guitar, etc.— in order for these to be seen differently. De la Sota's constructions did not begin with but rather moved toward the visual and "familiar": he *projected* appearance, and form was arrived at through the particularity of its construction.

The "image" of the Maravillas Gymnasium was formed by the extension of an existing upper courtyard onto the roof, a sectional solution that allowed both light and air into the sports hall and the classrooms. Architecture and structure were thus bound together, constructing and structuring each other. The structuring of the project relied on its fabrication, as much as its fabrication relied on its programmatic, sociological, economic, material, and technological circumstances.

6.11

Alejandro de la Sota,

Maravillas Gymnasium, Madrid, 1962.

Since the circumstances of each project are different, de la Sota felt obliged to invent new solutions for each building. What remained constant in all his projects, nevertheless, was his commitment to using new techniques as enabling frameworks for architecture. He did not adopt technology in a totalizing or dominating manner, but rather utilized specific techniques to modify and subsequently invent new forms of spatial relations. The uniqueness and the particularity of each solution resists or interrupts the otherwise subjugating logic of abstract technology.

The design for the residential college in Orense (1967) exemplifies this last point clearly. De la Sota proposed the use of repetitive structures made of prestressed concrete with different interior finishes and housing different functions. The smaller components—windows, doors, etc.—were based on details from the railway and coachwork industry. Adapting the repetitive units to the sloping terrain, the suspension of a single abstract datum, allowed him to transform the constructive logic of the modules, as did his recognition of other vernacular constructions of Galicia, his homeland.

Working in this way, de la Sota avoided the pitfalls that have become common in contemporary practice: he designed buildings which, despite their uniqueness, express something of the everyday, of the anonymous world of industrial products, of other houses, gymnasia, and offices. In a world so eager for representation, this architecture seems justly poised between reticence and invention, dedicated to a sense of the real that mere representations neglect.

CHANCE CONSTRUCTION

The use of brick in some of de la Sota's early projects bears a resemblance to the work of Sigurd Lewerentz, and in particular to the church of St. Mark in Björkhagen, Sweden (1956–1960). In many respects, the brickwork of St. Mark has the quality of being stretched over the undulating surfaces of the building. Lewerentz deliberately selected a deep red brick so that the white trunks of the nearby birch trees would be clearly delineated against the building's surface. Lewerentz had a deep understanding of building construction and was determined to have the builders follow correct procedures and methods. A case in point was his insistence that masons would not be permitted to join the project until they were sufficiently familiar with the writings of Hjalmar Granholm, the professor who had written an influential dissertation on masonry techniques. But

6.12
Sigurd Lewerentz,
church of St. Mark,
Björkhagen, Sweden, 1960.

Lewerentz's knowledge of building technique did not prevent the occurrence of accidents, nor his recognition of their value.

The external skin of the church achieves a specific spatial quality partly through its oscillating wall; but the building can equally be read as a mold or a carving, the solid residue of an implied outer perimeter that occasionally extends into its interior. Despite this reciprocity between the inside and the outside, Lewerentz was intent on keeping the surfaces continuous and flowing. His use of frameless insulating glass windows illustrates this intent, for the glass rests on brackets fixed to the outside wall and is sealed around the edges. Lewerentz further developed this method in the church of St. Peter in Klippan a few years later (1963–1966). Here the effect of this glazing system, however, places more emphasis on the undulating planarity of the external skin. From the very beginning of the Klippan project, Lewerentz had intended to have the brickwork sandblasted to achieve a smooth surface. For this purpose, he and his masons experimented with many different mixes of mortar to obtain the correct surface quality after sandblasting. However, toward the end of the project he decided to leave the wall in its rough form. In fact, Lewerentz seems to have valued the effects of chance occurrences throughout the construction period, despite the fact that he worked carefully and with exactitude. Thus, his architecture acknowledges the unconventional and the irregular, the deformed.

An example of this approach is his decision not to use cut bricks, which changed the mortar spacings throughout the building. The three rules that guided the construction process were (1) to use brick for all types of surfaces—floors, walls on the inside and outside, and occasionally for the ceilings as well; (2) to use only standard brick and tiles; and (3) not to cut bricks or tiles. This practice led to great variety, even irregularity, not only in mortar widths but in surface patterns as well. Combined with his apparent restrictions on the use of plumb lines and spirit levels, these rules of building sustained an architecture of discrepancies similar to Alejandro de la Sota's, an architecture of adjusted standards, or imperfections—compelling as an image because it was not designed as one.

AS FOUND

Even though Nigel Henderson's photographs of the East End of London emphasized the fragmentary and in many respects cinematic experience of urban life, the architecture of the Smithsons, despite the diversity of its materials, still

6.13
Sigurd Lewerentz,
church of St. Peter,
Klippan, Sweden, 1966.

6.14
Sigurd Lewerentz, church of St. Peter,
Klippan, Sweden, 1966.

presented the wholeness and coherence of a single building. In the work of de la Sota this coherence is challenged to a great degree, particularly in his Maravillas Gymnasium, where the juxtaposition of the roof section with the skin of the building creates volumetric projections and recessions that are highlighted through the use of different materials, with the result that a singular reading of the building is not possible. Perhaps the building that most productively explored the erosion of the singular and coherent volume, both conceptually and literally, was Stirling and Gowan's Engineering Faculty building at Leicester University (1959–1963). In this building, as in the collages of Paolozzi and the readymades of Duchamp, there is an acceptance of "found" objects and their transformation. But not only materials and surfaces are juxtaposed; entire volumes are as well. In other brutalist projects, the primary use of one material, concrete, led to a greater differentiation of parts, the much-studied example being Le Corbusier's monastery of La Tourette of 1953–1957. Despite the regularity of its cell arrangements, other parts of the monastery—the refectory, chapel, library, etc.—are expressed in separate and volumetrically distinct figures, as if it were a three-dimensional montage. The same could be said of the Leicester building, but Stirling and Gowan did not limit their materials to concrete. Juxtaposed in this case are the volumetric enclosures of distinct functions: laboratories on the ground floor and (in different forms) on upper levels, lecture theaters, and small rooms for administration. The juxtaposition is also structural, for each volume has its own manner of bearing loads.

Yet, while the Leicester building's volumes are articulated as distinct, each is given greater material consistency. The most important materials are brick, tile, and glass (both transparent and opaque). While used distinctly, they are not used typically; for example, the typical associations of solidity and support for brick are not reinforced by its use on the building's surfaces. Peter Eisenman has observed that the same is true for the transparent glass, which "often seems substantial, and opaque glass the reverse," a reversal that calls into question "the nature and meaning of the other dominant pair of materials—brick and tile."[10] Despite Stirling's empirical claims regarding materials in this building, they are used in ways not solely determined by their pragmatic role. An example is the inclined, prismatic windows of the laboratory building, which are projected out and in front of the plain surface of the brickwork. Glass, typically a thin surface, is in this case three-dimensional and appears to be solid, while the brickwork has the planarity of a sheet of glass. Kenneth Frampton described the building's use of patent

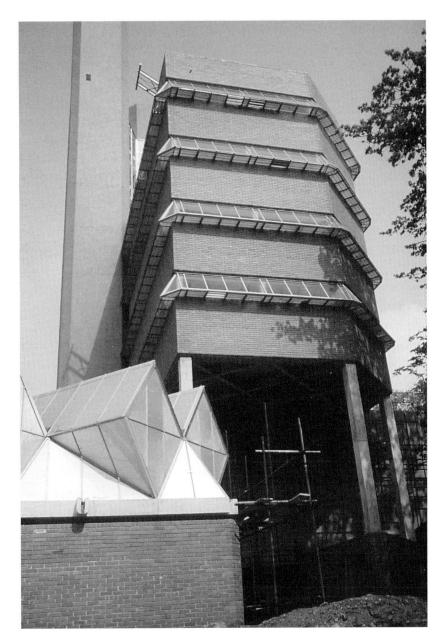

6.15
James Stirling and James Gowan,
Faculty of Engineering building,
University of Leicester, Leicester, 1963.

glazing "as a *matière* whose spectacular qualities are to be most effectively revealed by draping it, like a giant curtain over a configured shell; a seductive form of material expression, on occasion . . . irrelevant to an intrinsic syntax of a particular structure."[11] Regardless of Frampton's valorization of "intrinsic syntax," particularly in relation to the aspirations of modernism, his observations reveal an approach in this building that negates the systematic use of coplanar, point-by-point correlations between structure and skin. This misfit between the building's structure and surface is not yet a "free surface," for the curtain still aligns with and conforms to the basic configuration of the structure, but these misalignments point the way to the possible autonomy of the surface.

The Engineering Faculty building does not present a singular unity of surface; rather, the simultaneous presence and proximity of the different building volumes with their various coverings are what provide its sense of appearance. Stirling demonstrated his awareness of this when he wrote, "Buildings are seen as mass from the distance but are seen as assemblage when close to. 'Expression of assemblage' is achieved through the visual articulation of each unit in the wall, optically assisted by adjoining units having contra-diagonal ribbing on their surface and also by the plane edge margins outlining the edge of the units. These edge margins are also necessary to give protection to the ribbing, particularly when units are being moved in the factory and transported and handled on site."[12]

The ambivalence regarding "mass" and "expression of assemblage" also works in another way, however. Stirling and Gowan's building is at once a compaction of distinct volumes, recollecting a series of partially recognizable forms from history, as if a catafalque or perhaps a frozen still life, and yet also allows itself to be read as an assembly of fragments. In discussing the details of the workshop area, Stirling drew an analogy between the superimposition of the right-angled and distorted (45-degree) glass planes of the skylight and a cubist image.[13]

During this period, axonometric drawings played an important part in the conceptual development of many of Stirling and Gowan's projects. A modernist device, this manner of drawing was used as much for representation of assembly as for disassembly. Its capacity to demonstrate how things are put together was used at Leicester to construct a project made up of a number of fragments held in balance. In fact, the axonometric drawing is the only means of experiencing the ensemble as a whole, rather than in terms of its elevations. Unlike many traditional facades, the three-dimensional outlines of these buildings are not limited

6.16
James Stirling and James Gowan,
Faculty of Engineering building,
University of Leicester, Leicester, 1963.

to the two-dimensional traces of an elevation; instead there are recordings of sectional profiles and changes in the buildings' depth of field. The elevation as a mechanism of signification is thus destabilized.

In Stirling and Gowan's later buildings, such as the History Faculty building at Cambridge University (1968), the distinctness of the individual volumes is lessened in favor of a more unified mass, creating not a singular object but one that is faceted and compacted. The building's compaction is strengthened by the limitation of materials to two: brick and glass. The glass plays a major role in this and serves to define the building's major volume, while the brick serves a framing or bracketing function.

The play of elements in the History Faculty building recalls nineteenth-century glazed engineering structures—railway stations, market and exhibition halls. But in its volumetric overlapping and the reflections and refractions of its surfaces, it recalls early twentieth-century cubist images. This parallel between industrial engineering and cubism has been present in architecture since the 1920s; Sigfried Giedion's *Space, Time and Architecture* was one of the most influential formulations of this interpretation. Stirling's comments on perceptual distance and movement share Giedion's notion of "space time," within which the reception of the building is also dependent on movement in and around it. Once perception is temporalized in this way, the unity or closure of the building is delayed: "Giedion deferred cognitive closure indefinitely and kept the process—like Le Corbusier's domino skeleton—'eternally open,' the subject forming and perceiving space while being formed by and for it."[14] With its completeness or closure delayed, the building takes on radically different characteristics; like the images of the new painting, those of the buildings Giedion envisaged would "open the empire of the anorganic and formless."[15]

FORMLESSNESS

Formlessness has been a pressing concern of much subsequent architecture, particularly when architects turned away from the images of modernity that Stirling's projects still acknowledged. There are many similarities between the nonorthogonal, fragmentary, nonfrontal, and surfaced characteristics of Stirling and Gowan's buildings of this period and the buildings of Frank Gehry, for example. Fragmentation is particularly apparent in Gehry's early residential buildings. In some of these projects, this quality results from the enclosure of different functions in individual but interconnected pavilions. Like the Leicester building, the design of these projects seems to have followed a two-step procedure: division of the functional program into distinct parts and the assembly of those parts into a workable whole—suppressing their connections and accentuating their individuality. But the similarity to Stirling and Gowan's work stops there, for Gehry's early work makes no reference to the forms and motifs of early modern architecture (Melnikov, Le Corbusier, etc.) but instead refers to the building's specific location, particularly its qualities of light. Gehry called the Los Angeles vernacular an "urban junkyard," emblems of which demonstrate the piecemeal or aggregate character of an urban assemblage. In part, his buildings imitated this assemblage.

Gehry's own house in Santa Monica, begun fifteen years after Stirling and Gowan's building at Leicester was completed, is a very good indication of his early practice of aggregating distinct elements. The fact that the project involved additions and alterations to an existing house might suggest the inevitability of a composite or hybrid set of forms. But whereas most projects of this kind envisage unity or wholeness as a result, this one preserves and celebrates the independence or autonomy of its constituent parts.

The construction of the building contributes to its incomplete or unfinished character. Familiar materials are used—timber studs, corrugated sheet metal, and chain-link fence—but they are used in unfamiliar positions, displaced. The positioning of each seems to have resulted from a series of accidents or improvisations, as if the "process" character of the work unfolded through a number of spontaneous acts that neither anticipated nor recalled the project's becoming. Gehry stressed the "handmade" character of this and other early buildings, arguing less for the banality of the materials than for their appropriateness to his knowledge of construction, which at the time was limited.

Gehry also proposed comparisons between his way of working and contemporary artistic practices, such as the flat-bed paintings of Jackson Pollock, the aggregate images of Robert Rauschenberg, or the assembled constructions of Joseph Cornell. Connections can also be made to the group of artists who became preoccupied with the "American ordinary"—Richard Hamilton, Robert Irvin, and David Hockney—painters whose work lacked the perfection and finality of the pop versions of the ordinary. Their aim was to allow familiar things to obtain new meanings through unlikely juxtapositions, not for the sake of some narrative, as in surrealist painting, but for the possibilities that arise out of the things themselves, in their banality. Here again Stirling's work seems a useful comparison, as does the architecture of Peter and Alison Smithson and the work of the British artists who were similarly engaged with everyday conditions and materials, Paolozzi and Henderson.

But the parts that were assembled in Gehry's Santa Monica house were not only "ordinary," isolated and displaced, they were fragmented—it was not the building that was fragmented, but its parts. The outer surface of the Santa Monica house can be called a second skin, for it wraps around the stud framing of the original house. But if "skin" is taken to mean a surface that is complete in itself and enveloping, it is here a misleading term. This building's second surface is continually, but unexpectedly, interrupted or broken by local incidents, discrete events: a bit a chain-link fence here, the corner of a window there, and so on. The consequence of this series of interruptions and agglutinations is that both unity of composition and completeness of containment are continually deferred, as if the building site were to remain a work site, as if the two were really the same thing.

This deferred or incomplete characteristic of the building's surface was to change in Gehry's later buildings, for what had been true of each surface became characteristic of the entire house. In his Winton guest house (1987), for example, the parts that have been assembled are not elements of construction (screens, apertures, coverings, and so on) but inhabitable volumes, as if the house were a collection, grouping, or ensemble of rooms. Yet here, too, wholeness is postponed. In Gehry's account, this house was decisive: "The breakthrough for me in this house was the idea of cracks between the buildings, wedge-shaped cracks that serve to differentiate the parts of the pure forms and suggest that they are complete forms because of this cleavage."[16] Fragmentation still exists, not in the constructed body of the building but rather in its volumes, each of which is complete in itself. Because each part is clad in a different material—limestone, brick, sheet metal, Finnish plywood, and so on—the unity or wholeness of the building remains indefinite. Gehry's account of observing aspects of the building in a sequence of views is a proposal for a kind of synthesis, but it is a perceptual synthesis, the responsibility of the spectator, not of the building. If Gehry's earlier house can be compared to a sculpture by Boccioni, the Winton guest house is like a still life by Morandi: a fragmented whole versus whole fragments. The unity that obtains in perception takes for granted the close adjacency of the figures, indifferent to their hidden, but adequate, functional interdependence.

6.17
Frank O. Gehry,
Guggenheim Museum, Bilbao, 1997.

A third way of composing "formless" buildings can be seen in Gehry's later and (now) more famous buildings. Beginning with the Team Disneyland Administration Building of 1987 or the Vitra Furniture Museum begun in the same year, the color coding of distinct volumes was replaced by a uniformity of surface treatment. While the several distinct volumes (rooms) of the earlier buildings have here coalesced into one, the geometry of the surface(s) becomes even more fragmentary, agitated, and insistently nonorthogonal. But this fragmented surface is not a composite construction. The cladding has become much more consistent, almost dogmatically so, limited to one or two materials, colors, and finishes. In these cases one can indeed speak of an enveloping surface, an outer covering that disavows traditional distinctions between front and back, top and bottom, ends and middle, as if the object (or the aggregation of fragments) were all of a piece, unified in itself and then inserted into its location (the Weisman Museum in Minneapolis, the Guggenheim Museum in Bilbao, the Neue Zollhof in Düsseldorf, and the Experience Music Project in Seattle). Again, the surface is no longer composed of fragments of construction, nor is the building an assembly of distinct volumes; instead, the patchwork of panels that makes up its surface is composed of pieces that have been cut from the same cloth, giving the building's novel geometries great regularity and cohesion. Thus, the strained unity of the early projects is replaced by a highly cultivated compositional synthesis. The use of the term "formless" to describe these buildings is thus appropriate only if comparisons are made with buildings that exhibit traditional geometries, for the unity that results from these surfaces is nothing other than "formal": form that intends to be original, nonreferential (to place or program), spectacular in its chromatic and luminous effects, and insistently coherent.

In 1960 Reyner Banham ended his *Theory and Design in the First Machine Age* with the following observation:

> It may well be that what we have hitherto understood as architecture, and what we are beginning to understand of technology, are incompatible disciplines. The architect who proposes to run with technology knows now that he will be in fast company, and that, in order to keep up, he may have to emulate the Futurists and discard his whole cultural load, including the professional garments by which he is recognized as an architect. If on the other hand, he decides not to do this, he may find that a technological culture has decided to go on without him. It is a choice that the masters of the Twenties failed to observe until they had made it by accident, but it is the kind of accident that architecture may not survive a second time.[1]

Such an alternative must have seemed dramatic, perhaps even extreme, to Banham's contemporary readers. Mies van der Rohe's Seagram Building had been finished just two years before, in 1958. Apart from a few detractors, such as Lewis Mumford, most critics judged it to be a great achievement as both an urban and technological solution. With this building in mind, Banham's comments would seem to be overstated.

In many of his designs, beginning with the glass skyscraper projects of the 1920s and again in his later high-rises, Mies attempted to find a path that was not as dualistic as that suggested by Banham. He repeatedly asserted that technology was not an end in itself but always intertwined with its metaphysical and symbolic values. In full conformity to arguments raised in his writings, his projects are evidence of the attempt to *transform* the facts of modern production into the act of symbol building.

7.1

Ludwig Mies van der Rohe,
Seagram Building, New York, 1958.

It is well known that in "Skyscrapers" Mies speaks of tall buildings under construction as "revealing the bold constructive thoughts"; yet he also emphasized the necessity for these structures to demonstrate something more than technical skill. For Mies, achieving this "something more" meant that the architect "would have to give up the attempt to solve a new task with traditional forms; rather one should attempt to give form to the new task out of the nature of this task."[2] Given the fact that steel frames were now carrying the load of the building, the external skin no longer needed to be structural. In skyscrapers, therefore, the use of glass provided new opportunities and would require new approaches.

Mies's Lake Shore Drive apartments and Seagram Building represent solutions that are quite different in nature. The floors and columns of the first are covered in steel, to which the mullions are welded, while the second has a curtain wall that is set in front of the load-bearing frame. The Seagram Building has a greater continuity of the skin—brown-tinted glass—across its face, the external membrane masking the structural frame behind.[3] The building's simple volume together with its uniform outer surface give it a sublime or monumental presence within its context.[4] (The building can also be seen as representative of the Seagram Corporation, of its role in the market and contemporary life.) That its monumental expression was not the result of technical considerations alone is apparent in the fact that Mies adjusted the articulation of the frame to preserve its uniformity and the building's volumetric simplicity. The choice of bronze and tinted glass added to this effect of melancholic solemnity. Mies made similar adjustments to the facades of the Lake Shore Drive apartments, acknowledging the role of the buildings' visual effect as decisive in the design of their cladding system. This explains his affinity to Berlage, as well as his somewhat paradoxical similarity to the approach of Venturi and Scott Brown. Yet, even though such buildings were expressive of the epoch's technological essence, they were also to be seen in symbolic terms, relying on the qualities of glass in ways that directly relate transparency to concerns of context, culture, and circumstance.

DISTRACTION

From the early period of his work onward, Mies remained preoccupied with the reflections produced by glazed surfaces. In the Lake Shore Drive apartments, this play of light and shadow resulted in a wall that presented changing appearances throughout the course of the day and one's movement around it. Such a building is at once a simple and somber prismatic mass and at the same time the locus of an unlimited series of spectral effects, which contribute as much to the building's "disappearance" as its appearance. Here it is useful to recall the arguments made by Siegfried Kracauer in his discussion of Berlin picture palaces, where he introduced the experience of "distraction"—a special form of looking, focused not on permanent figures nor on entire objects but on local or minor occurrences, and thus attentive to the ephemerality of urban phenomena.[5] Urban density made this form of looking possible, as did mass society and mass communication. The play of reflections across the Seagram Building's curtain wall could be understood as an architecture of "distraction." Seen thus, its glass and bronze are manifestations not only of technical reason but of the urban and cultural conditions of the time—conditions that recognized movement as a key experience. Buildings seen in this "distracted" way, like films, present figures that are variously black and white, opaque-transparent-reflective, or sharply outlined and ambiguous. Their darkness, opacity, and mass not only make them sublime, or "terrific," but give them a sense of monumentality, the past, and history. Their lightness, reflectivity, and surface ambiguity, however, give them a contemporaneity, even a future, because they acknowledge the agency of technological progress.

In the years and decades after the construction of the Seagram Building, many similar office buildings were erected in metropolitan centers. In one sense, this imitation could be seen as a vindication of Mies's assertions about the technological character of the epoch: conditions that his buildings were meant to express sustained the development and production of countless others. But in the majority of these later buildings, the design was primarily driven by technical and economic imperatives. Little attention was paid to matters of monumentality, even less to the elements of distraction. And with the neglect of monumentality came indifference to considerations of history, to previous expressions of the character of the epoch.

In 1962, a few years after the completion of the Seagram Building, José Luis Sert discussed the influence of curtain walls for office buildings, which he saw as evidence of "Americanization" in the remotest of cities. Sert dismissed these structures as "facades of anonymity" designed to serve the average bureaucrat regardless of his job or his preference for privacy, view, or sunlight.[6] To him, the fact that the curtain wall could be arranged through the repetition of one

7.2
Skidmore, Owings and Merrill,
Lever House, New York, 1952.

window type was equivalent to playing a guitar with one string. Against this type of structure and the kind of modernism it implied, Sert turned to vernacular or traditional building. The functions of the window (ventilation, view, and light) could be managed together in one aperture or separately, through the use of different elements. These are practical matters, acknowledged within a given context of building production. Sert was, of course, part of the modern tradition, but he was also part of the group that wanted to reconsider the premises of early modernism and introduce into contemporary architecture a reevaluation of the past. The problem Sert faced was observed by many: that of overcoming the dullness and anonymity of postwar modernism by reconsidering the practical and figurative aspects of traditional building, while using contemporary materials and methods.

In the design and criticism of the late 1960s and 1970s, architects and theorists who were sensitive to the issue of the building's temporality pursued two considerations: how to find an architecture and urbanism that would restore connections to the cultural inheritance; and how to discover a manner of building that would visibly communicate its adherence to anteceding architectures, thus easing anxiety about the meaning or meaninglessness of contemporary building.

MODERN BUILDING AND HISTORICAL MEMORY

History could be, and often is, seen as a phenomena of change, of epochs and associated styles succeeding one another in time. Another conception was operative during the 1970s, however, especially in Italy, where the laws or permanent forms of architecture and urbanism were being discovered and proposed as an alternative framework for design. An important figure in this period was Saverio Muratori, a theorist and historian of cities, whose studies of Venice and Rome guided many later projects. Particularly important was his dedication to the idea that urban architecture conformed to laws or exhibited recurring types.

The renewed interest in typology, which began during the 1960s, was an attempt to address simultaneously issues of repetition and of historical continuity in architecture. It was argued that the history of architecture resembled that of other useful crafts and instruments. Thus, like "a basket or plate or cup, the architectural object could not only be repeated, but also was meant to be repeatable."[7] The inherent logic of repeatability denied the uniqueness of the architectural object and linked the project with reproduction.

In the arguments about architectural type, which derived from Enlightenment thinkers such as Quatremère de Quincy, the distinction between type and model was once again emphasized: "The word 'type' represents not so much the image of a thing to be copied or perfectly imitated as the idea of an element that must itself serve as a rule for the model. . . . The model, understood in terms of the practical execution of art, is an object that must be repeated as it is; type, on the contrary, is an object according to which one can conceive works that do not resemble one another at all. Everything is precise and given in the model; everything is more or less vague in the type. Thus we see that the imitation of types involves nothing that feeling or spirit cannot recognize."[8]

For advocates of typological theory, the type-model distinction also related to their criticism of mass production insofar as it, like the model, dealt with the exact repetition or copying of an object (normally taken to be an original, in the sense of a prototype). The type, by contrast, allowed for a more fragmentary and metaphorical connection to ideas or "structures" that were not so much technical but associative and thematic. Quatremère's interests were metaphysical, concerned with the essence of architecture as well as with principles. If the repetition of models in mass production neglected history, the rediscovery of type would be the means of recovering it, and with it a sense of meaning or of life. Yet, given the "essential" character of type, the question of the building's actual appearance or the communication of meaning raised considerable anxiety. Although Quatremère did not propose the idea, those seeking a communicative architecture—one that would replace the dull anonymity of mid-century modernism—discovered forms in history that seemed to have a constancy equivalent to the constancy theorists had attributed to types. This "case for figurative architecture," however, distorted both Quatremère's position and Muratori's, just as it attempted to overcome the modernist support for repetition through mass production.[9]

Aldo Rossi claimed that architecture lies at the interface of memory and reason. Types were thought to preserve the reason of form, but they were also seen as the objects of recollection, even of longing: "behind feelings I searched for the fixed laws of a timeless typology."[10] This search assumes that types exist outside of time, unlike the functional programs with which they are associated when built. Rossi based his "critique of naive functionalism" on a separation of type from its concrete manifestation and sought to preserve that distinction, knowing full well that the pressures of life and of "locus" would militate against it. The separation between the type and its manifestation gives to the cities and buildings resulting from the assembly of type forms an overwhelming sense of emptiness and absence, much like the "metaphysical" settings of Giorgio de Chirico. Rossi's reflection on the Lichthof in Zurich suggests, however, that emptiness was less important than a sense of potential—the potential for inhabitation—made apparent when life is "suspended." If types communicate, they do so through the events that may occur within the settings they establish, not through the forms they present. This "may occur" sustains the "vagueness" of type proposed by Quatremère.

Others, however, associated the conventionality of type with a form of arbitrariness that provides the architect with the freedom to establish an ideological position through the decisions taken in the manipulation of forms. These decisions give the project its specificity or singularity. Accordingly, considerations of program are not foreign to working with types and become necessary prerequisites of the project's ideological content. Does Rossi's atemporal view of the recollection of types propose a sense of history that is distinct from the historicity of an ideologically motivated or context-bound project?[11]

If one conceives history as a succession of discrete events, often called "linear time," then memory represents a different understanding of urban and architectural temporality. The two examples of permanence introduced by Rossi can clarify the way he conceived history. There are, in his account, two kinds of permanence in urban settlements, those of housing and of monuments. Both persist "through" time, but in different ways: housing (as distinct from the individual house) remains the same despite changes in the particular details and aspects of some of its elements, while the physical body of each monument remains the same despite changes in its ambient milieu. Both give cities their durable and identifiable character. Yet in this, too, Rossi described a duality: permanence can be either pathological or propelling. This last distinction is important, as it provides a key to his conception of history. The permanences that are "propelling"—monuments like the Palazzo della Ragione in Padua—are no longer defined by their original function; they escape linear time or history because they have accommodated many functions over time. The past and present that they have subsumed into their form anticipate future occupations. This makes the building, or its image, less a chronicle than a story, even a fiction, which is also the subject matter of "analogical thinking." Canaletto's well-known painting of three Palladian projects is for this reason a key to Rossi's designs and arguments, for it clearly shows how times and places that have been freed from the chains of temporal succession can be joined together because of their atemporal typological relatedness to one another. Conjunctions between architectures of different times thus put an end to history, but also open up the possibility of recollection. At this point, Rossi's "scientific" research into urban history becomes autobiographical, for the memories that prompt analogical connections are always one's own.

Autobiography, however, is not the final word in this argument. Autonomy, or the uncontaminated rationality of architectural research into types, always confronts places and materials that have concrete specificity. The succession of functions that each type sustains is always bound to a unique topography, a locus. The series of functions and modifications is thus also something singular. The autonomous contains within itself the potential for collective understanding. Memory, not history, builds out of the ahistorical understanding of types the promise of their reappropriation in specific times and places through the fictions of analogical imagination.

This understanding of history and memory gives the building's surface both poverty and potential. It is no doubt fair to describe the surfaces of Rossi's buildings as silent and cold: he himself promoted this characterization. But this is no failing. The same, he thought, could be said of the buildings of Adolf Loos, and before him of the projects of Boullée. There is no desire to communicate or signify in Rossi's work if that means to represent some content other than the architecture itself. Rafael Moneo has observed that "architecture is the sole protagonist of [Rossi's] work, and it is *architecture* that he presents us with again and again, whatever the program or the circumstances in which it is produced."[12] Thus, the fact that his buildings do not signify this or that content does not mean they are senseless, nor that they cannot be seen as "images." But they must be seen as images that reflect one another within the play of analogical reference. They reflect the form of historical substance that is intrinsic to architecture: "Rossi always situates a new work in the context—the landscape—of his own complete work; it has become a sort of framework for an architecture of desire, which on the other hand, maintains the attributes of anonymity and generality that belonged to the architecture of the past."[13] Surfaces such as those of the Gallaratese Quarter or the Modena cemetery make no great effort to signify. These surfaces are determined by the realities of construction in a specific place,

7.3
Aldo Rossi, housing,
Gallaratese Quarter, Milan, 1970.

nothing of which is sentimental but all of which sustains recollections that may, in time, reconstruct the public domain.

Rossi went on to teach at the ETH in Zurich in the early 1970s, where he continued to espouse his thoughts for a younger generation of architects. In their distinction from the purely sociological and psychological approaches of the other professors, Rossi's ideas provided something different, something new. He told his students, among them Jacques Herzog and Pierre de Meuron, that architecture is always architecture and that social and psychological disciplines cannot substitute for it. Rossi's emphasis on the production of architecture, on drawings, and on the world of the imagination replaced the democracy of neighborhood data collection with the permanence of monuments and his treatise on architecture and the city. But despite his suspension of history as a category, in preference for the past as a domain of sedimented materiality, much of Rossi's architecture of this period has a nostalgic and melancholic quality. This quality was of course partly intentional but also may have been the trap of an architecture that could not escape the unavoidable slippage of type into model, for one of the most difficult tasks of architecture is determining how to negotiate its relationship to the past as part of its project of becoming—its future.

This topic is intertwined with the work of Herzog and de Meuron and their de facto rejection of tradition as an instrumental mechanism for architectural projection. For Herzog and de Meuron there is more uncertainty than comfort in reproducing what has been in the past. According to Herzog, "Ten or twenty years ago, modernism was still hoping for a new modern tradition and postmodernism offered to remake imagery from past eras. But today making an object is a new problem each time. What is theater? What does a window look like?"[14]

REPRESENTATION AND NONREPRESENTATION

Rossi's lessons were received therefore with a degree of skepticism by Herzog and de Meuron, who did not wholly forget the role of the sociological and psychological. More importantly, perhaps, they did not forget the perceptual qualities of things. Architecture is an artifice whose phenomenal attributes are its primary means of engaging and activating its connections with its users. Rossi's praise of the virtues of stability in the American town, articulated at the beginning of the first English edition of *The Architecture of the City,* affirms the representational and valorizes the images conveyed by monuments of these towns. In some respects no less representational, the outer skins of many buildings by Herzog and de Meuron are dependent on the clear understanding of the artificial nature of materials. This mode of construction more often than not first begets a momentary, visceral response before it conveys the rationality of its logics. The forms and the surfaces of their buildings also work, therefore, in ways that are nonrepresentational in comparison to those of Rossi, whose early work in particular literally re-presents, albeit in reductive fashion, an idealized and symbolic architecture. The scenographic characteristics of much of Rossi's work in the 1970s constitute a reenactment of the past as a backdrop for contemporary events—for the present. The appearance of his architecture, probably more than that of any other architect of this period, managed to negotiate the line between modernism and classicism. Compare, for example, the elementary school at Fagnano Olna (1972–1976) to the secondary school at Broni (1979). Even though both projects rely predominantly on symmetrical plan arrangements, the surfaces of these buildings are rendered planar and white, punctured only by the recesses of windows and doors. The overall effect, however, oscillates between modernity and tradition, even if—in the case of the Fagnano Olna school in particular—that tradition is the architecture of Adolf Loos. The combination of reductivism with geometrical and symbolic ideality reinforces the monumental character of these buildings, linking them again to Loos's interpretation of architecture as a tomb or monument.

The aloofness of Rossi's synthetic architecture does not, according to Rafael Moneo, allude to any stylistic tendencies: "Rossi's effort as an architect is to abandon and to consign to oblivion all that could be labeled stylistic, because for him architecture is not accessory, nor that which can be added. On the contrary, architecture is all those things that man builds in his absolute defenselessness."[15] But it is important to recognize that Rossi's attempt to construct an anonymous architecture is itself an intellectual, not a literal, project. Anonymity is both a stylistic category and a result of recollection: mimesis. "Mimesis is better understood insofar as it is a reproduction of that which already exists. It is hard to think of mimesis, even in classical terms, without being aware of the existence of a world of recognized and conscious fiction."[16]

Mimesis in this sense—reproduction achieved through recognition and based on image and form—is, in the work of Herzog and de Meuron, replaced by a mimesis of materials and production procedures. But unlike the relationship of functionalism to the imperatives of mechanization, this work contains a montage of industrial products. Instead of a one-to-one correlation between purposive industrial elements and their corresponding architectural image, Herzog and de Meuron consider surface effects as part of the material and constructional palette of a project. In this way their works question the space between functional necessities and ornament, contingencies and supplement, inasmuch as most of their built projects produce effects that are either additions to or iterations of the logic of repetitive production.

At the Ricola storage building (1986–1987), for example, the Eternit cladding panels are larger at the top than at the bottom. These sloping panels are surmounted by a cantilevered timber structure that reveals the galvanized sheet-metal box on the building's inside. For the architects, the visual references of this building are "the traditional stacking of sawn timber boards around the numerous saw mills of the area, as well as the limestone quarry within which the storage building sits."[17] The mimetic power of this building and others is based on the specific situation of production and the circumstances of each project rather than on the image of an earlier architecture. For Herzog and de Meuron, the processes and procedures of production become the key components of a work's imagibility.

Their more recent library at Eberswalde (1996) explores the relationships between image and construction more literally. For this building, the architects worked in collaboration with the photographer Thomas Ruff. A series of newspaper photographs Ruff had collected were chemically transferred to and impressed on the building's concrete surfaces. Its prefabricated panels show a photographic image that is repeated horizontally sixty-six times, like a film reel. There are seventeen rows of panels (with some images taking up more than one row). The combination and narrative sense of these still images are dependent on viewpoint and light. Accordingly, they allow for visual motion or stillness. The sgraffito type of process used for the transference of images to the surface of this building is not additive, like printing, but rather works by erasing or scratching the surface. This technique is common for the application of geometric patterns onto DIY panels as well as for the decoration of Alpine farmhouses. Herzog and de Meuron's technique was more refined, however, for they experimented with and controlled the drying times of concrete for the clarity of the pixelated images.

7.4

Herzog and de Meuron,
La Ricola storage building,
Laufen, Switzerland, 1987.

7.5
Herzog and de Meuron,
Senior Technical School library,
Eberswalde, Germany, 1996.

The work of Herzog and de Meuron is emblematic of many strands that have developed in the period after postmodernism, strands that differ in many interesting ways but share a doubt about the sort of signification or meaning proposed in that architecture. This is not to say there is no concern with the building's image, but references to previous architecture are not what is being offered. Nor does this trend signal a return to early modern architecture, if that is assumed to treat materials and construction as the basis for a building's image. Today an increasing number of architects are becoming concerned with construction, materials, and processes, but they do not assume that technology will "determine" the image, in the old sense of functionalism. Although Banham warned that architects who did not "run with" technology might be left behind, recent projects show that the alternative is not so simple.

The doubt about functional determinism is linked to a suspicion about the role of any particular material—say glass—in representing what is new about an epoch. Instead, the question focuses on what is possible with such a material. This possibility is further enhanced by research into new types of glass, the properties of which play an important role in constructing unprecedented architectural and spatial effects. Thus, glass has changed: now, for example, it can be used as a transparent, translucent, or opaque material; it can be used structurally; its colors can be exploited, as can its capacity to receive and filter inscribed images. And these uses are not the only ones that have been discovered. Similarly unexpected uses result from new combinations with other materials. Glass, then, is not only a sign of an epoch but a topic of research. Its operative possibilities have replaced its role as a signifier. The same is true for other materials, both new and old.

POSTSCRIPT

In a time when almost all of the elements used in the building process are pre-made in a factory or workshop, architectural construction has become a process of assembly. No longer does site labor involve the cutting, joining, and finishing of "raw materials"; instead it entails the installation of components that have been preformed and prefabricated somewhere other than the building site. Construction these days tends to be largely a dry not a wet process, the elements of which are not only precise and exact but meant for specific assembly procedures.

These techniques intend the construction of a *system,* an integrated unity that is characterized by (1) the functional interdependence of parts, (2) internal intentionality, and (3) independence from territorial obligations. The functioning of a glazing system, for example, depends on these conditions: first, on the interdependence of its mechanisms of operation—fasteners, sealants, sheets of glazing, etc; second, compatible performance standards for each of the parts; and, third, the relative autonomy of the ensemble, which allows it to be used in different locations. Although relatively recent as an achievement of building construction, the idea of such a composition has ample precedent in both architectural theory and its philosophical and scientific sources.

One of the most influential early formulations of the idea that the elements of a system are dependent on one another was set forth by Immanuel Kant: "I consider a system to be the unity of manifold knowledge under one idea. This is the idea formed by the reason of the form of a whole, in so far as such a concept determines *a priori* both the size and the position of the parts in respect to each

P. I

Willem Dudok, Town Hall,
Hilversum, Netherlands, 1931.
Photo: Charles H. Tashima, 1991.

P.2
Gio Ponti with Pier Luigi Nervi,
Pirelli Tower, Milan, 1960.
Photo: Charles H. Tashima, 1991.

other. The scientific concept of the reason, therefore, contains the end [or functional purpose] and the form of the whole. . . . Thus, the whole is articulated, not heaped together; it can grow from within, like the body of an animal, whose growth does not add a limb, but makes every limb stronger and fitter for its purposes without changing the proportion."[1] The difference between this conception of ensemble and an aggregate is that the interdependence of the parts is governed by an idea. Wholeness in this sense resembles Leon Battista Alberti's notion of *concinnitas,* a unity from which no part could be taken without weakening or destroying the whole. But for Kant the regulative principle, the functional or purposive nature of the system, was key: "purposive unity (*Zweck-mässigkeit*) was a regulative principle in nature . . . [as if or assuming that] the idea of unity had been her [nature's] foundation."[2] Later writers on art and architecture argued similarly about works of artifice. The functioning, performance, or operations of a building were seen to depend on the coordination and internal cooperation of its component parts.

In functionalist arguments, the idea of a system's purpose received great stress, so much so that these parts were said to "determine" nonpurposive concerns, such as style or figuration. This did not always mean that form was to follow function, but that overall shape, like purposiveness, was to be integral and consistent. The aesthetic qualities of an "organic" composition necessitated the perfect unity of parts.

Yet the organic approach was not without its critics in the late nineteenth and twentieth centuries. Aesthetic unity and the closure it implies have been criticized by writers and designers in favor of fragmentation and the *opera aperta.* The philosophical foundation for key aspects of this debate was set out Martin Heidegger. His role is somewhat ironic, for many now see him as a conservative in matters of art and politics. Nevertheless, for Heidegger this desire for "gathering together," this dedication to unity, is precisely what typifies the "enframing" that has come to be characteristic of our technological age—an age that not only he but Herbert Marcuse, Jürgen Habermas, and Arnold Gehlen have seen as a threat to human existence.[3]

Are "systems" of building construction a "threat" to the lives that are meant to be accommodated in buildings?

When explaining his rather unusual sense of the German word *Gestell* (enframing), Heidegger first elaborated the implications of its prefix, comparing the gathering of elements in such a framework to the collection of mountains in

P.3

Jože Plečnik, Križanke Monastery
restoration, Ljubljana, 1956.

P.4
Luigi Moretti, Uffici e Abitazioni,
Milan, 1957. Photo: Charles H.
Tashima, 1991.

P.5

Antonio Comini, Palazzo Bonacossa,
Milan, 1894. Photo: Charles H.
Tashima, 1991.

a mountain range (*Gebirg*) and of feelings in one's disposition (*Gemüt*). The prefix *ge-* is important because it signifies "gathering together." The collection and integration of elements on a bookshelf or in a skeleton are both signified by the word *Ge-stell*.[4] But it is not the unity of parts in such an ensemble that makes Heidegger's sense of enframing unusual and difficult, nor is this what makes the *Gestell* threatening. For Heidegger the term *Stell* means a setting upon or standing forth. Every *Stellen*, he observed, is a standing forth, a placement, positioning, or imposition. This sense of the word is apparent in the German word *Dar-stellen*, meaning presentation. The peculiarity of technological enframing is that it is a positioning or standing that is also a "challenging forth," a pro-duction, that draws or tears "out of concealment" the resources of the earth, conferring upon them the status of a "standing reserve." This transforms the earth into material, a commodity, which makes the constructed work less the outcome of care or cultivation than of exploitation.

Even if we accept this sense of technology, the difficulty of Heidegger's account is not overcome, however, for he also maintains that the enframing that defines modern technology is related to the "bringing forward" that occurs in art and poetry, because both poetic and technological disclosure are productive and revealing. Yet, unlike poiesis, enframing is a "challenging which puts to nature the unreasonable demand that it supply energy that can be extracted and stored as such," exposing and ordering it to "stand by," ready to be used and eventually used up. This is the "danger" of technology.

For many readers, these observations have prompted a reactionary response: to avoid the danger of exhausting the environment, the forward march of modern technology must be halted. This sentiment is particularly evident in contemporary ecological theory and environmental ethics, where Heidegger's arguments on technology have surprising currency and are used to buttress the alternately alarmist and pious arguments for conservation and "letting be" (Heidegger's *Gelassenheit*). Whether or not one shares this ethics and politics, it clearly poses some difficulty for architecture, because a new building cannot result from "letting things be." Heidegger himself stressed the *productive* character of art, particularly architectural art. As long as architecture is understood to augment reality by establishing what it naturally lacks, architecture must be understood as essentially akin to technology. Even though most architects realize that the two cannot be separated, many take a position for or against technology. Even when

P.6

Herzog and de Meuron,
Suva Building, Basel, 1993.

P.7

Georges Chedanne, 124 Rue Réaumur,
Paris, 1905. Photo: Charles H.
Tashima, 1991.

P.8
MVRDV, Huis KBWW, Utrecht,
1997.

the alternative is avoided, we are often presented with an odd mixture of confidence and doubt: blind enthusiasm for the newest methods and techniques coupled with profound inability to agree on the limits, even aims, of their use. Viewed more broadly, the continued faith in the advances of modern technology is paralleled by a corresponding doubt about its use. It is not that most doubt technology, or reject its results (for few critics are willing to relinquish the newest means), but many doubt our ability to deploy these results and methods responsibly, which is why it is impossible to ignore the current debate on environmental ethics.

The other reason that architecture and technology are difficult to separate is that both involve *foresight;* both involve the intelligence implied in the nongraphic sense of the term "making plans." Plans of this sort are made by architects, politicians, and tourists—by all of us. Does our tendency to rely on plans, forecasts, and predictions pose a problem?

In his criticism of the common assumption that technology is essentially a matter of contrivances or instruments, Heidegger introduced the related concepts of cause, "occasioning," and "bringing forth." Technology is not essentially a matter of devices or machines, but the knowledge that exists in advance of something "coming forth," serving in part as its agency. This knowledge also exists in architecture, for part of the intellectual labor of project-making is the understanding that proposes and governs building construction. The building itself is anticipatory; its parts are prepared for some occurrence in natural or human affairs. Because anticipatory thinking cannot be divorced from human understanding, the alternative between technology and anthropology proposed in much reactionary criticism cannot be sustained.

TECHNIQUE

The centrality of technological thought to both human understanding and architectural imagination has been the subject of much speculation. One story of the origin of the arts, which is also the origin of human existence, suggests that they came into being as a result of the same series of mythical events.

All arts and techniques were given to the human race by Prometheus. Of the versions of this story that survive from antiquity, the account set forth by Plato is for our purposes the most useful:

P.9
210 Spuistraat, Amsterdam.
Photo: Charles H. Tashima, 1991.

P.10
Kallman, McKinnell and Knowles,
City Hall, Boston, 1967.

P. 11
Renzo Piano and Richard Rogers,
Pompidou Center, Paris, 1977.
Photo: Charles H. Tashima, 1991.

Once upon a time, there existed gods but no mortal creatures. When the appointed time came for these also to be born, the gods formed them within the earth out of a mixture of earth and fire and the substances which are compounded from earth and fire. And when they were ready to bring them to the light, they charged Prometheus and Epimetheus with the task of equipping them and allotting suitable powers to each kind. Now Epimetheus begged Prometheus to allow him to do the distribution himself—and "when I have done it, you can review it." . . . In his allotment he gave to some creatures strength without speed, and equipped the weaker kinds with speed. . . . [Thus, giving to each its powers,] he made his whole distribution on a principle of compensation, being careful by these devices that no species should be destroyed. . . .

Now Epimetheus was not a particularly clever person, and before he realized it he had used up all the available powers on the brute beasts, and being left with the human race on his hands unprovided for, did not know what to do with them. While he was puzzling about this, Prometheus came to inspect the work, and found the other animals well off for everything, but man naked, unshod, unbedded, and unarmed, and already the appointed day had come, when man too was to emerge from within the earth into the daylight. Prometheus therefore, being at a loss to provide any means of salvation for man, stole from Hephaestus and Athena the gift of skill in the arts, together with fire—for without fire it was impossible for anyone to possess or use this skill—and bestowed it on man.[5]

The story begins with the topic of proportion: Epimetheus was to give to each species its due power, speed to some, strength to others, and so on. In the allotment, however, he forgot the human race. This forgetting is the first introduction of the problem of knowledge into the story. At this stage, three points merit emphasis: (1) humans are similar to animals because they are formed "out of the earth," (2) humans are different from animals because they were left out of the initial proportioning of "natural" powers, and (3) before they were given fire and the arts, humans, as such, did not exist. Next came Prometheus, and following his arrival a rapid series of decisive events. After the fault of neglect came the theft, which resulted in a gift, the gift of that power which distinguishes the human race: art, technique, or "sly thought." Here the account of origins collapses on itself, for the gift was presupposed in the giving: the theft itself was an instance of "clever" thought, of foresight, or of technique.

P.12
Jean Nouvel, Cartier Foundation,
Paris, 1994.

P.13
Louis H. Sullivan,
Carson Pirie Scott building,
Chicago, 1904.

P. 14

Michel de Klerk and P. L. Kramer,
De Dageraad housing,
Amsterdam, 1922.

The tale concludes with a series of consequences of the fault and gift. First, the use of fire and of the arts led the human race to develop religious practices, language, clothing, and houses—each of which was an artifact that in some ways covered the nakedness that defined humans before they were humans. The next consequence was that shortly after the human race settled itself in groups they learned they could not defend themselves against attack, for they had not learned the art of war, nor of politics. They tried to protect themselves by forming cities, but failed again because they lacked political skill. This led to another gift, perhaps the greatest of all. Observing their failures and fearing their destruction, Zeus sent Hermes to the human race in order to teach them a sense of justice, which would allow them to bring order to their cities. Concluding his story, Protagoras stressed that the sense of justice was bestowed upon all individuals equally, no matter what art they practiced, whether farming or financing.

The story describes two faults and two gifts: Epimetheus and Prometheus were responsible for the first two, Prometheus and Zeus for the second. Why this division, or how are we to understand the promise and weakness of technical know-how? Epimetheus is a name that signifies "knowing after the fact," hindsight. This understanding was demonstrated by the not-so-clever realization of the need for humans to be given their "powers." Prometheus, by contrast, is a name that signifies foresight (*pro-mathein*). He is the hero of prescience, of anticipation, of what is to come. In this narrative, his foresight was apparent in his grasp of what the underprovisioned humans would require to satisfy their needs, fire and the arts. Although beneficial, his foresight was incomplete, for even with his gift human existence was still wanting in its lack of political skill. Thus the gift of justice (from Zeus through Hermes), by which cities were established. This story suggests that cities and by implication architecture will not result from technical modalities of understanding alone.

In what way is technical knowledge incomplete, incompletely human and incompletely prescient? On first thought, it would seem that the first gift was a supplement: neglected by Epimetheus, people were naked. Le Corbusier, too, imagined "original" nakedness in his account of the interdependent beginnings of the human race, arts, and language. In his *Talks with Students,* he observed that "folklore," or prescientific knowledge, "shows us 'man naked,' dressing himself, surrounding himself with tools and objects, with rooms and a house, reasonably satisfying his minimum requirements and coming to terms with the surplus to permit him the enjoyment of his great material and spiritual well-being."[6] Does

P.15

Max Bill, Hochschule für Gestaltung,
Ulm, 1953.

P.16

Matthias Sauerbruch and Louisa Hutton,
GSW Building extension, Berlin, 1998.

P.17
Adolf Krischanitz, New World School,
Vienna, 1994.

this mean that at their origin—when naked—humans were already fully human, complete as such? This idea would suggest that the instruments of dressing were both supplementary and accessory, which is to say nonessential, like ornaments draped or inscribed on a building's primary enclosure or "white walls." The Prometheus story implies, however, that the thesis of original nakedness is false; before the gift, before art, humans had not yet appeared "out of the earth." In the time before art, the human race was not only neglected but unknown. Fire, and with it the arts, allowed mankind to come into existence, to emerge from within the earth and stand up or out in the daylight. On this point the Promethean myth parallels Plato's parable of the cave. Heidegger observed that technological understanding uncovers, is a matter of disclosing or revealing. Because the human race is not entirely part of the animal or natural world, man-ufactured instruments are the means by which the human race comes into being.

Thus, what may seem to be a supplement is actually constitutive: the arts and instruments of language, dressing, and architecture are not added to naked bodies but constitutive of them. Before language, clothing, and architecture, the human race was not yet human, only potentially so. And like the bodies they constitute, these artifacts *stand out* in order to define what is human. This rela-tionship is expressed clearly in the word *prosthesis,* which signifies something that is placed in front of, or outside of, something else. In this instance, however, what is outside the body is also what makes it what it is. There is thus no "original" nakedness in human existence. The life of a human being involves being outside oneself. Before technique, humans were "without qualities," with neither pros-pect nor possibility.

Insofar as prosthetics enable art, they also inaugurate human temporality. Instruments anticipate, prepare, or propose something to be done, enacted, or performed. Prometheus was the hero of foresight, of expectation. The same is true of the instruments he gave the human race: tools and the know-how their use assumes enable all manner of performances, for each tool allows one to expect some result or consequence. And no occurrence of this kind is natural. Thus, artworks, instruments, and prosthetics compensate for nakedness, whereas pre-mature existence is defined by a lack of qualities. Epimetheus's effort was compensatory.

Prometheus lacked access to the citadel of Zeus because he lacked under-standing of the whole or of justice, which would contribute to the good of the whole. Thus, the origin of art is also the prompting of labor, for the many arts

P.18

Adolf Krischanitz, New World School,
Vienna, 1994.

P.19

Office building, Santiago, Chile.

are all examples of knowledge that involves actual projects or work. And work can be successful or not. Prometheus was aware of this, because his foresight was a promise of failure: "I knew—and yet not all." Technique inaugurates human history because the foresight of its proposals is always somewhat lacking; each eventually fails. Every failure, great or small, gives rise to a new task, and thus to the history of similar performances. Every tool of language, clothing, and building is both a memory and a project. Technical operations demonstrate foresight and planning, but this foresight recognizes past traces of neglect. Failure prompts projects, and every new production proposes a recuperation.

Bernard Stiegler has described the "posterity" of technical objects as that of sustaining their own "naturalization" or appropriation into what has arisen non-technologically.[7] One agency of this "naturalization" is the "territory" neglected by the "autonomy" or internal definition of the technical system—an agency of obvious potential and inevitability in the making of an architectural "system."

In the last pages of Heidegger's reflections on enframing, he describes technological modalities of thought as a matter of "danger." These modalities block the appearance of truth, the subject matter of poetic disclosure. But this observation does not prompt him to reject technology. Enframing, he said, is a "prelude" to its opposite, to "the event of appropriation."

APPROPRIATION

What would characterize such an "event of appropriation" in a technological age? In fact, its characteristics have already been indirectly proposed: it would be nonpropositional or improbable, and it would be territorial or territorially specific. Also characteristic of such an event would be the discovery of similarities, which had been deferred by technical knowing. This would be the discovery of unforeseen relationships among individuals, among ensembles or systems, with one another and with what had not been planned.

Architectural surfaces consist not only of instances of "internal intentionality" or autonomy—for example, Mies's primitivism, Albert Kahn's Fordism, or Jean Prouvé's "closed systems"—but also of situations in which similarly systematic premade objects and processes are appropriated into nontechnical conditions. In many cases there are instances of movement back and forth between technical and nontechnical conditions. In these cases, elements or systems enter into *play* with conditions of human praxis and location: parts that were planned to "work" independently are reworked in dialogue with the conditions of the project. The premade parts that were selected to perform certain roles are reworked in order to play different roles: what had been deferred in design is acknowledged in construction and use, as if what had been premade were of necessity remade. So, too, with the materials of construction. If one puts in abeyance assumptions about "the nature of materials" and about their natural meanings (which are certainly as much associational as natural), one can see how construction can be a process whereby improbable uses are discovered to yield new, and newly significant, meanings. Misuse can lead to reuse and new use, as is apparent not only in the work of Lewerentz and de la Sota but also in that of the Smithsons and Jean Nouvel. Here, as before, design projection is only a partial determination; equally effective or participant in the historical process are improbabilities of place and performance. And these "agencies" of appropriation unfold through time, a time of partial successes and partial failures.

Each device or technical apparatus, then, is a chronicle of its own modification, a proposal that is discovered to be "not so clever," which is followed by a recuperative and appropriating reproposal that is itself, eventually, discovered once again to be incomplete. Such a discovery is a consequence of both partial foresight and changed circumstances, no matter whether one judges these circumstances to be a punishment or a gift, threatening or emancipating. Regardless of such a judgment, this "history" cannot be escaped. Nor is it insignificant, for it is precisely this history that gives to the surface its identity as the site of a performance, of both a people and a place. This history also gives to the construction its signifying substance, as a prominently visible evidence of care (in construction and reconstruction), which in architecture can be defined as the tragic labor of reconciling foresight with neglect.

NOTES

I INTRODUCTION: WHY SURFACE ARCHITECTURE?

1. Albert Kahn, "Architectural Trend," *Journal of the Maryland Academy of Sciences* 2, no. 2 (April 1931), 124–125; cited in Terry Smith, *Making the Modern: Industry, Art, and Design in America* (Chicago, 1993), 81–83.

2. Alan Colquhoun, "The Concept of Regionalism," in G. B. Nalbantoglu and C. T. Wong, eds., *Postcolonial Space(s)* (New York, 1997), 17.

3. Kenneth Frampton, "Towards a Critical Regionalism: Six Points for an Architecture of Resistance," in Hal Foster, ed., *The Anti-Aesthetic* (Port Townsend, Wash., 1983), 16–30.

2 FRAMING CONTAINMENT

1. On this problem, see studies of Renaissance architecture such as Wolfgang Lotz, *Studies in Italian Renaissance Architecture* (Cambridge, Mass., 1977); Rudolf Wittkower, *Gothic versus Classic* (London, 1974), and others; as well as more recent studies of perspective, especially Robert Klein, *Form and Meaning* (New York, 1979), and Hubert Damisch, *The Origin of Perspective* (Cambridge, Mass., 1994). Two facades that illustrate this point are those for San Lorenzo in Florence and San Petronio in Bologna. The history of early attempts at the "beautification" of buildings through facade treatment is described in Wolfgang Braunfels, *Mittelalterliche Stadtbaukunst in der Toskana* (Berlin, 1953), chapter 2 especially.

2. On the expression of the passions in the eighteenth and nineteenth centuries, see most recently Jennifer Montagu, *The Expression of the Passions* (New Haven, 1994).

3. Robin Middleton, introduction to Nicolas Le Camus de Mézières, *The Genius of Architecture; or, the Analogy of That Art with Our Sensations* (Santa Monica, 1992), 28.

4. Ibid.

5. On this development and Ledoux's theories in particular, see Anthony Vidler, *Claude-Nicolas Ledoux: Architecture and Social Reform at the End of the Ancien Régime* (Cambridge, Mass., 1990),

206–207 especially. For Le Camus de Mézières and his role in this argument, see Robin Middleton's introduction to *The Genius of Architecture*. The early eighteenth-century development of character is set forth in Donald Drew Egbert, "Character," in *The Beaux-Arts Tradition in French Architecture* (Princeton, 1980), 121–139. See also Joseph Rykwert, *The First Moderns* (Cambridge, Mass., 1980).

6. See Manfredo Tafuri on "speaking architecture" in *Architecture and Utopia* (Cambridge, Mass., 1976). See also Jean Starobinski, *1789: The Emblems of Reason* (Charlottesville, 1982); Anthony Vidler, *The Writing of the Walls* (Princeton, 1987); Vidler, *Claude-Nicolas Ledoux;* and Hans Sedlmayr, *Art in Crisis* (London, 1957). On prisons and their signification, see Robin Evans, *The Fabrication of Virtue* (New York, 1982); and more broadly, Michel Foucault, *Discipline and Punish: The Birth of the Prison* (Harmondsworth, 1977).

7. Le Corbusier, *The Decorative Art of Today* (Cambridge, Mass., 1987), 190. See also Mohsen Mostafavi and David Leatherbarrow, *On Weathering: The Life of Buildings in Time* (Cambridge, Mass., 1993); and Mark Wigley, *White Walls, Designer Dresses* (Cambridge, Mass., 1995).

8. Etienne-Louis Boullée, *Architecture: Essay on Art,* in Helen Rosenau, *Boullée and Visionary Architecture* (London, 1976), 106.

9. Ibid.

10. Philip Johnson and Henry-Russell Hitchcock, *The International Style,* reprinted in *Functional Architecture* (Cologne, 1995), 14–18.

11. Paul Zucker, "Planning in Three Dimensions," in Zucker, ed., *New Architecture and City Planning* (New York, 1944), 4.

12. Sigfried Giedion, "The Need for Monumentality," in Zucker, ed., *New Architecture and City Planning,* 552.

13. Ibid., 555.

14. Ibid., 553.

15. Joseph Hudnut, "The Post Modern House," *Architectural Record* 97, no. 5 (May 1945), 70–75.

16. Quoted in Sigfried Giedion, *Architecture, You and Me* (Cambridge, Mass., 1958), 48–52; previously published in *Architektur und Gemeinschaft* (Hamburg, 1956), 40–42.

17. José Luis Sert, *Can Our Cities Survive?* (Oxford, 1944), 232–233.

18. José Luis Sert, "Centres of Community Life," in J. Tyrwitt, J. L. Sert, and E. Rogers, eds., *The Heart of the City* (New York, 1952), 13–14.

19. Louis Kahn, "Monumentality," in Zucker, ed., *New Architecture and City Planning,* 578.

20. Louis Kahn, "Order Is," in *Louis I. Kahn: Writings, Lecture, Interviews,* ed. Alessandra Latour (New York, 1991), 58–59; first published in *Perspecta* 3 (1955).

21. On the relationship between the anonymity of mass production and the necessity of uniqueness, see Richard Sennett, *The Fall of Public Man* (Cambridge, Mass., 1976), 142–145. Sennett discusses how the early department stores created exotic settings for the exhibition of mass-produced items as a way of distancing the products from their conditions of production. In this argument Sennett elaborates Karl Marx's concept of "commodity fetishism."

22. On the philosophical and sociological implications of anonymity, see Maurice Nathanson, *Anonymity* (Bloomington, 1986), 23–44 especially.

23. Rosalind Krauss, "The Double Negative: A New Syntax for Sculpture," in *Passages in Modern Sculpture* (Cambridge, Mass., 1983), 243–288.

24. Robert Morris, "Some Notes on the Phenomenology of Making: The Search for the Motivated," in *Continuous Project Altered Daily* (New York, 1993), 73.

25. Hans Frei, *Konkrete Architektur? Über Max Bill als Architekt* (Baden, 1991).

26. Alfred Roth, *The New Architecture* (Zurich, 1946), 178.

27. On the development of these ideas, see Jean-Louis Cohen, *Scenes of the World to Come* (Paris, 1995).

28. This account of aesthetic meaning was set forth by Herbert Read in *Art and Industry* (Bloomington, 1953), 37–41: "Roger Fry once doubted whether a typewriter could ever be beautiful, but in recent years new designs for typewriters have been evolved which are infinitely better in shape and appearance than previous models, and though one might still hesitate to call them works of art, they are certainly progressing in that direction."

29. Colin Rowe, "Chicago Frame," in *The Mathematics of the Ideal Villa and Other Essays* (Cambridge, Mass., 1976), 90.

30. Louis Sullivan, *The Autobiography of an Idea* (New York, 1956), 314.

31. Ibid.

32. Claude Bragdon, *The New Image* (New York, 1928), 89.

33. This point, made in opposition to conclusions reached by historians of Chicago architecture and urbanism such as Lewis Mumford, has been stressed by Daniel Bluestone in *Constructing Chicago* (New Haven, 1991), in the introduction especially but elsewhere throughout.

34. Sullivan, quoted in Claude Bragdon, *The Frozen Fountain* (New York, 1932), 28ff.

35. Louis Sullivan, *Kindergarten Chats* (New York, 1979), 187 and 207.

36. John Root, "A Great Architectural Problem," in *The Meaning of Architecture* (1890; New York, 1967), 141.

37. Montgomery Schuyler, "A Critique of the Works of Adler and Sullivan," *Architectural Record* (December 1895), 3–48.

38. Frank Lloyd Wright, "The Art and Craft of the Machine," in *Frank Lloyd Wright Collected Writings*, vol. 1, ed. Bruce Brooks Pfeiffer (New York, 1992), 64–65.

39. John Zukowsky, ed., *Chicago Architecture and Design, 1923–1993* (Chicago, 1993), 214ff.

40. Le Corbusier, *When the Cathedrals Were White* (New York, 1964); Erich Mendelsohn, *Amerika* (Berlin, 1928).

3 WINDOW/WALL

1. Le Corbusier, *Precisions* (Cambridge, Mass., 1991), 51.

2. Le Corbusier and Pierre Jeanneret, "Five Points towards a New Architecture," in Ulrich Conrads, ed., *Programmes and Manifestoes on 20th-Century Architecture* (London, 1970), 99–101.

3. Le Corbusier, *Precisions,* 60.

4. Le Corbusier, *The Radiant City* (New York, 1967), 41–64.

5. Le Corbusier, *Une petite maison* (Zurich, 1991). For a discussion of the spatial implications

of the horizontal window, see Bruno Reichlin, "The Pros and Cons of the Horizontal Window," *Daidalos* 13 (1984), 65–79.

6. Le Corbusier, *Une petite maison,* 5 and 9.

7. Le Corbusier, *Precisions,* 59.

8. Reichlin, "The Pros and Cons of the Horizontal Window."

9. See Kyra Stromberg, "Das Fenster im Bild, das Bild im Fenster," *Daidalos* 13 (1984), 54.

10. Le Corbusier, *Oeuvre complète 1929–1934* (Zurich, 1947), 66–71.

11. Ibid., 144–153. For a full account of this design, which alludes to the views Le Corbusier has chosen to illustrate, see Peter Carl, "Le Corbusier's Penthouse in Paris: 24 Rue Nungesser-et-Coli," *Daidalos* (1987), 65–71.

12. On this argument see Neil Levine, "Questioning the View: Seaside's Critique of the Gaze of Modern Architecture," in David Mohney and Keller Easterling, eds., *Seaside: Making a Town in America* (New York, 1991), 240–259.

13. Although this phenomenon was developed in much of modern painting, perhaps the most eloquent and instructive case is Picasso's *The Women of Algiers* (1955), as described by Leo Steinberg in "The Algerian Women and Picasso at Large," in *Other Criteria* (London, 1976), 125–234.

14. On the subject of openness in this sense, the classic text is Umberto Eco, *The Open Work* (Cambridge, Mass., 1989), especially chapters 1–4.

15. An excellent text on this and other Matisse window paintings is Clara Gottlieb, "The Role of the Window in the Art of Matisse," *Journal of Aesthetics and Art Criticism* (Summer 1964), 393–423. A shorter version of the argument put forth in this article is contained in Clara Gottlieb, *The Window in Art* (New York, 1981). An equally useful account of this motif in painting is J. A. Schmoll gen. Eisenwerth, "Fensterbilder," in *Beiträge zur Motivkunde des 19. Jahrhunderts* (Munich, 1970), 13–166. This subject in modern painting is examined in Suzanne Delehanty, *The Window in Twentieth-Century Art* (Purchase, N.Y., 1986).

16. Just as pespectival space can be seen as a "symbolic form," so can the space of "postperspectival" constructions. On perspective in this sense, see Erwin Panofsky, *Perspective as Symbolic Form* (New York, 1991). The preface to this edition by Christopher Wood puts Panofsky's argument in its historical context. Two studies of perspective that have elaborated and deepened Panofsky's are Robert Klein, "Perspective and Scientific Speculations in the Renaissance," part 2 of *Form and Meaning* (New York, 1979); and Hubert Damisch, *The Origin of Perspective* (Cambridge, Mass., 1994), especially part one. The philosophical implications of Panofsky's text have been developed in Maurice Merleau-Ponty, "Eye and Mind," in *The Primacy of Perception* (Evanston, 1964), 159–192. Because Merleau-Ponty's study treats modern as well as Renaissance painting, this article adds to our understanding of paintings like this one by Matisse. Perspective as a "constructed" symbolism has been considered in view of modern philosophy by Karsten Harries, "Descartes, Perspective, and the Angelic Eye," *Yale French Studies* 49 (1973), 28–42. The "constructed" nature of "realities" such as perspective is demonstrated by David Lachterman, *The Ethics of Geometry* (New York, 1989), especially part one, "Construction as the Mark of the Modern."

17. Albrecht Dürer, *The Painter's Manual* (1525; New York, 1977), 434. This image was discussed by Panofsky and some of the authors mentioned in the preceding note; but for the full

historical context of this image, see Erwin Panofsky, *The Life and Art of Albrecht Dürer* (Princeton, 1955). For our purposes, a useful interpretation of this image, as it relates to the work of Marcel Duchamp, is set forth in Rosalind Krauss, "The Story of the Eye," in *New Literary History* 21, no. 2 (1990).

18. The argument that Leonardo is the artist who discovered anamorphosis is set forth in Carlo Pedretti, *Studi vinciani* (Geneva, 1957). A more generalized account in English is set forth in Carlo Pedretti, *Leonardo* (New York, 1985), 271–289 especially. Pedretti's argument is related to the history of studies of perspective in Klein, "Perspective and Scientific Speculation in the Renaissance." The relationship between Leonardo's pioneering work in anamorphosis and the later tradition is demonstrated in Martin Kemp, *The Science of Art: Optical Themes in Western Art from Brunelleschi to Seurat* (New Haven, 1990). Also useful on Leonardo's role in the early history of anamorphosis is Erwin Panofsky, *The Codex Huygens and Leonardo da Vinci's Art Theory* (London, 1940).

19. The basic text on anamorphosis is Jurgis Baltrušaitis, *Anamorphic Art* (Cambridge, 1977). Also useful is Gustav René Hocke, *Die Welt als Labyrinth* (Hamburg, 1957), especially chapters 17 and 21.

20. Karl Fleig, ed., *Alvar Aalto, the Complete Works,* vol. 1 (Zurich, 1963), 134–135. See also Karl Fleig, *Alvar Aalto* (New York, 1975), 93.

21. Theo van Doesburg is most explicit on the qualities of "anticubic" architectural space. See, for example, Theo van Doesburg, "Towards a Plastic Architecture," in Conrads, ed., *Programmes and Manifestoes on 20th-Century Architecture,* 78–80. Additional aspects of this argument, or this concept of space, are put forward in "The New Architecture and Its Consequences," in Joost Baljeu, *Theo van Doesburg* (New York, 1974), 142–147, 189–198. The historical context within which these arguments emerged is set forth in H. L. C. Jaffé, *De Stijl, 1917–1931* (Cambridge, Mass., 1986); and Mildred Friedman, ed., *De Stijl, 1917–1931: Visions of Utopia* (Oxford, 1982). See also Kenneth Frampton, *Modern Architecture: A Critical History* (London, 1980), 142–149.

22. On the role of performance in architecture, see Homa Fardjadi, "Delayed Space: Performance and the Labors of Architecture," in *Delayed Space: Work of Homa Fardjadi and Mohsen Mostafavi* (New York: Princeton Architectural Press, 1994), 12–17.

23. Linda Nochlin, "*The Cribleuses de Blé:* Courbet, Millet, Breton, Kollwitz and the Image of the Working Woman," in *Malerei und Theorie: Das Courbet-Colloquium 1979* (Frankfurt, 1980), 52.

24. C. M. Armstrong, "Edgar Degas and the Representation of the Female Body," in Susan Rubin Suleiman, ed., *The Female Body in Western Culture: Contemporary Perspectives* (Cambridge, Mass., 1986), 237.

25. Jacques Derrida, *The Truth in Painting* (Chicago, 1987), 54.

26. Reichlin, "The Pros and Cons of the Horizontal Window."

27. Frampton, *Modern Architecture: A Critical History,* 107.

28. On Muzio and these buildings in particular, see J. Mascai and P. Doukas, "Expressed Frame and the Classical Order in the Transition Period of Italy, 1918–1939," *Journal of Architectural Education* 40, no. 4 (1987), 10–17; and Giuseppe Gambirasio and Bruno Minardi, eds., *Giovanni Muzio: opere e scritti* (Milan, 1982), 154–159.

29. Mascai and Doukas, "Expressed Frame and the Classical Order."

30. The critical literature on this building is extensive; most useful are Hermann Czech and Wolfgang Mistelbauer, *Das Looshaus* (Vienna, 1976); Burkhardt Rukschcio and Roland Schachel, *Adolf Loos: Leben und Werk* (Salzburg, 1982); and Benedetto Gravagnuolo, *Adolf Loos: Theory and Works* (Milan, 1982). On "rationalism" in Loos's works, see Aldo Rossi's introduction to Gravagnuolo's book and to the Italian translation of *Das Andere, La civiltà occidentale* (Bologna, 1981). See also three books by Massimo Cacciari: *Adolf Loos e il suo angelo* (Milan, 1981); *Dallo Steinhof* (Milan, 1980); and most recently, *Architecture and Nihilism* (New Haven, 1993), 161–166.

31. Adolf Loos, "Men's Fashion," in *Spoken into the Void: Collected Essays 1897–1900,* trans. Jane O. Newman and John H. Smith (Cambridge, Mass., 1982), 11.

32. Ibid., 12.

33. Adolf Loos, "Weiner architekturfragen," in *Trotzdem* (Innsbruck, 1931).

34. This passage is cited in F. Michael Sharp, *The Poet's Madness* (Ithaca, 1981), 73–75. On the philosophical implications of this stance, see Paul Ricoeur, *Oneself as Another* (Chicago, 1992).

35. Karl Kraus, *Half Truths and One-and-a-Half Truths: Selected Aphorisms* (New York, 1986), 122.

36. Egon Friedell, *A Cultural History of the Modern Age,* vol. 3 (New York, 1954), 300; cited in Allan Janik and Stephen Toulmin, *Wittgenstein's Vienna* (New York, 1973), 97.

37. Adolf Loos, "Building Materials," in *Spoken into the Void,* 65.

38. Adolf Loos, "The Principle of Cladding," in *Spoken into the Void,* 66.

39. Adolf Loos, "Josef Veillich," in *Trotzdem.*

40. Czech and Mistelbauer, *Das Looshaus,* 108.

41. Pierre Chareau, "Une maison de verre," *Glace et Verre* 17 (1930), 19–20.

42. José Luis Sert, "Windows and Walls: An Approach to Design," *Architectural Record* 131, no. 5 (May 1962), 132–133; reprinted as "On Windows and Walls," in *José Luis Sert: Architecture, City Planning, Urban Design,* ed. Knud Bastlund (New York, 1967).

43. Ibid.

4 THE APPEARANCE OF COVERING

1. On this topic, see Werner Oechslin, *Stilhülse und Kern* (Zurich, 1994); Ákos Moravánszky, "The Aesthetics of the Mask," in Harry Francis Mallgrave, ed., *Otto Wagner: Reflections on the Raiment of Modernity* (Santa Monica, 1993); Mary McLeod, "Undressing Architecture," in Deborah Fausch et al., eds., *Architecture in Fashion* (Princeton, 1994); and Mark Wigley, *White Walls, Designer Dresses* (Cambridge, Mass., 1995).

2. Eduard F. Sekler, *Josef Hoffmann, the Architectural Work* (Princeton, 1985), 82–85; see also his essay "Structure, Tectonics, Expression," in György Képes, ed., *Structure in Art and Science* (New York, 1965), 89–95.

3. Sekler has pointed out that rope was used to frame windows in traditional Belgian buildings; see Sekler, *Josef Hoffmann,* 509.

4. Ibid.

5. On Fabiani, see Marco Pozzetto, *Max Fabiani: Ein Architekt der Monarchie* (Vienna, 1983), 65; and Boris Podrecca, *Max Fabiani: Bauten und Projekte in Wien* (Vienna, 1983).

6. See Pozzetto, *Max Fabiani,* 63.

7. On this aspect of pointillist painting, see David Leatherbarrow and Mohsen Mostafavi, "On Weathering: A New Surface out of the Tracks of Time," *Daidalos* (March 1992), 116–123.

8. The phrase "art of pure color" is John Root's; see Donald Hoffmann, ed., *The Meanings of Architecture: Buildings and Writings by John Wellborn Root* (New York, 1967), 176–186. In this essay, Root discusses the importance of color in architecture and praises the impressionists. Root's essay emerged in the context of much discussion of Semper in Chicago, led, perhaps, by Frederick Baumann, and Root's translation of a couple of Semper's shorter papers. Semper's article "On the Study of Polychromy and Its Revival" had been published in 1851, in *The Museum of Classical Antiquity,* 1, 228ff. Root's position can be understood clearly in the following rhetorical forecast by Semper: "Each wall surface or column gains new interest from its varied coloring. Soon the same beauty will cover every creation by the true artist in more lasting materials, and we will learn to forestall the witchery of time. . . . What will be accomplished in the street fronts of our houses will be more swiftly done upon the walls of our rooms."

9. Otto Wagner, *Modern Architecture,* trans. Harry Francis Mallgrave (Santa Monica, 1988), 84–85.

10. On the shift from one to the other, see Peter Haiko, "Otto Wagner's Interieurs: Vom Glanz der französischen Könige zur Ostentation der 'Modernen Zweckmässigkeit,'" in Julius Posener et al., *Otto Wagner* (Vienna, 1984), 34–46 especially.

11. Posener et al., *Otto Wagner,* 39; see also Mallgrave, ed., *Otto Wagner.*

12. On this point, see Edward Ford, *The Details of Modern Architecture* (Cambridge, Mass., 1990), 213–217 especially, from whose interpretation we have benefited.

13. Wagner, *Modern Architecture,* 93.

14. See Oechslin, *Stilhülse und Kern,* who described the similarities and differences between their approaches to cladding, and their relationships to Semper. This account includes a full treatment of their dependence on the arguments of other figures, particularly Karl Bötticher.

15. Gottfried Semper, *Der Stil in den technischen und tektonischen Künsten,* vol. 1 (Mittenwald, 1977), 231.

16. Ibid., 444; see also Wagner, *Modern Architecture,* 32. For a review of Semper's ideas on color, see Wolfgang Herrmann, *Gottfried Semper: In Search of Architecture* (Cambridge, Mass., 1984), 125–126 especially.

17. Harry Francis Mallgrave, introduction to Gottfried Semper, *The Four Elements of Architecture* (Cambridge, Mass., 1989), 40.

18. On the relationship between textile symbolism and community building in antiquity, see Indra Kagis McEwen, *Socrates' Ancestor* (Cambridge, Mass., 1993); on the relationship between architectural ornament and festival apparatus in remote antiquity, see George Hersey, *The Lost Meaning of Classical Architecture* (Cambridge, Mass., 1988).

19. Semper, *Der Stil,* vol. 1, 229; see also Semper, *The Four Elements,* 255–256; Hans-Georg Gadamer, *The Relevance of the Beautiful* (Cambridge, Mass., 1986), 57–65. The fictional and

productive character of mimetic objects is set forth briefly and clearly in Paul Ricoeur, "The Function of Fiction in Shaping Reality," in *Man and World* 12 (1979), 123–141.

20. F. W. J. Schelling, *The Philosophy of Art* (Minneapolis, 1989), 169.

21. For a comprehensive review of this and the development of the later tradition, see Kenneth Frampton, *Studies in Tectonic Culture* (Cambridge, Mass., 1996).

22. Owen Jones, *The Grammar of Ornament* (London, 1856), 13–14. See also Robert Goldwater, *Primitivism in Modern Art* (Cambridge, Mass., 1986). More broadly on tattoo, see Arnold Rubin, ed., *Marks of Civilization: Artistic Transformations of the Human Body* (Los Angeles, 1988). In architecture, the ancient topos for "marks of civilization" is the Vitruvian version of shipwrecked Aristippus, who saw in the geometry marked on the Rhodian shore traces of civilization; see Vitruvius, *Ten Books on Architecture,* book 6, preface.

23. Semper, *Der Stil,* vol. 1, 92ff.; see also Joseph Rykwert, *The Necessity of Artifice* (London, 1982), 139, note 54.

24. Alois Riegl, *Problems of Style* (Princeton, 1992), 75–79, figs. 31–32.

25. Ibid., 39.

26. Captain James Cook, *Journal of the First Voyage* (London, 1769).

27. See Georg Simmel, "Adornment," in *The Sociology of Georg Simmel* (New York, 1950), 340; see also Susan Stewart, *On Longing* (Durham, N.C., 1993), 127. For a full account of the range of meanings attached to the word "ornament," see Ananda Coomaraswamy, "Ornament," in *Traditional Art and Symbolism* (Princeton, 1977). Coomaraswamy himself included illustrations of Maori tattoos in "The Traditional Conception of Ideal Portraiture," in *Christian and Oriental Philosophy of Art* (1956), 116. The plate he selected, showing two portraits of a Maori chieftain, was from Leo Frobenius, *Das unbekannte Afrika* (Munich, 1923).

28. Rubin, ed., *Marks of Civilization,* 14.

29. On the difference between cooking and medicine, see Plato, *Gorgias* 501a ff.; on the difference between healthy and cosmetic beauty see *Hippias Major* 291a.

30. Adolf Loos, "Ladies' Fashion," in *Spoken into the Void: Collected Essays 1897–1900,* trans. Jane O. Newman and John H. Smith (Cambridge, Mass., 1982), 102.

31. Ibid.

32. Robert Venturi, "Diversity, Relevance and Representation in Historicism, or Plus ça change . . . Plus a Plea for Pattern All Over Architecture . . . ," the 1982 Walter Gropius Lecture, in *Architectural Record* (June 1982), 114–119.

33. Ibid., 116.

34. Robert Venturi, Denise Scott Brown, and Steven Izenour, *Learning from Las Vegas* (Cambridge, Mass., 1972), 64. Of the many, many commentaries on this book and more specifically on the idea of the decorated shed, we have found the most useful to be Stanislaus von Moos, "Anatomy of a 'Decorated Shed,'" in *Venturi, Rauch and Scott Brown* (New York, 1987), 22–31 especially.

35. Von Moos, "Anatomy of a 'Decorated Shed,'" 230.

36. Ibid.

37. Camillo Sitte, *Der Städtebau* (Vienna, 1910).

38. H. P. Berlage, "Bouwkunst en impressionisme," reprinted in *Architectura* 2 (1984), 93–95, 98–100, 105–106, 109–110. See also Manfred Bock, *Anfänge neuen Architektur* (Wiesbaden, 1983), 113–120. For an elaboration of these ideas as they relate to Sitte's ideas on city planning, see Vincent van Rossem, "Berlage and the Culture of City Planning," in Sergio Polano, *Hendrik Petrus Berlage* (New York, 1988), 45–65.

39. See Manfred Bock, Jet Collee, and Hester Coucke, *Berlage in Amsterdam* (Amsterdam, 1992), 28.

40. Leatherbarrow and Mostafavi, "On Weathering," 116.

41. See Charles Voysey, "The Aesthetic Aspects of Concrete Construction," *Architect and Engineer* 57 (May 1919), 80–82.

42. Ludwig Mies van der Rohe, "Skyscrapers," in Fritz Neumeyer, *The Artless Word: Mies van der Rohe on the Building Art* (Cambridge, Mass., 1991), 240.

43. Neumeyer, *The Artless Word,* 110.

44. Venturi, Scott Brown, and Izenour, *Learning from Las Vegas,* 79.

45. Ibid.

46. Karl Scheffler, *Moderne Baukunst* (Leipzig, 1908), 19.

47. Frobenius's well-known and widely circulated book contains sections devoted to particular territories in Africa, as well as to the whole country—an "Atlas Africanus." Each section treats characteristics of people and place (*Kulturmorphologie*) and attends in great detail to architectural concerns. Frobenius's argument is structured according to three ideas of the temple: the temple as nature, the temple as building, and the temple as world. While the buildings show an allegiance to "simple" construction methods, the ornaments demonstrate great variety and liveliness; one elemental subject, such as the human ear, is shown with a wide range of surface marks.

48. William Jordy, *American Buildings and Their Architects* (New York, 1976), 221–278.

49. Mies van der Rohe, "Skyscrapers," 240.

50. Jordy, *American Buildings and Their Architects,* 241.

51. Mies van der Rohe, "Architecture and Technology," in Neumeyer, *The Artless Word,* 324.

52. Mies van der Rohe, in "Mies van der Rohe's New Buildings," *Architectural Forum* 97 (November 1952), 99; cited in David Spaeth, *Mies van der Rohe* (New York, 1985), 130–131.

53. Robin Evans, "Mies van der Rohe's Paradoxical Symmetries," *AA Files* 19 (1990), 57–68.

54 On this building and on Kahn's work generally, see Federico Bucci, *Albert Kahn: Architect of Ford* (New York, 1993), 105ff.; Terry Smith, *Making the Modern: Industry, Art, and Design in America* (Chicago, 1993); and Grant Hildebrand, *The Architecture of Albert Kahn* (Cambridge, Mass., 1974).

55. Randall Ott, "Reflections on the Rational and the Sensual in the Work of Ludwig Mies van der Rohe," *Arris* 4 (1993), 38–53. Irony is especially evident in the collage showing the Egyptian Old Kingdom sculpture, if we recall that part of north Africa was occupied by German troops and therefore occasionally attacked by American bombers.

56. Colin Rowe and Robert Slutzky, "Transparency: Literal and Phenomenal," reprinted in

Colin Rowe, *The Mathematics of the Ideal Villa and Other Essays* (Cambridge, Mass., 1976), 159–183.

57. Anon., "Industrial Buildings," *Architectural Forum* (January 1942), cited in Bucci, *Albert Kahn,* 108.

58. William Fogg, "Daylight Illumination of Industrial Buildings," *Architectural Forum* (September 1929), 405–410.

59. Smith, *Making the Modern,* 78.

60. The departments in the firm's technical division designed the whole building. The work in all of the departments started at the same time, which resulted in speeding up the process of preparing the drawings and the specifications for all the trades. This allowed the submissions of all drawings at one time. If necessary, this procedure could result in the preparation of the drawings of a factory in less than ten days. See George Nelson, *Industrial Architecture of Albert Kahn, Inc.* (New York, 1939), 19–20.

61. Neutra's diagram is published in Richard J. Neutra, *Amerika: Die Stilbildung des neuen Bauen in den Vereinigten Staaten* (Vienna, 1930), 36.

62. Knud Lönberg-Holm and C. Theodore Larson, *Development Index: A Proposed Pattern for Organizing and Facilitating the Flow of Information Needed by Man in Furthering His Own Development, with Particular Reference to the Development of Buildings and Communities and Other Forms of Environmental Control* (Ann Arbor, c. 1953).

63. George Howe, "Flowing Space: The Concept of Our Time," in Thomas H. Creighton, ed., *Building for Modern Man* (Princeton, 1949), 168.

64. Smith, *Making the Modern,* 71.

65. Antonio Gramsci, *Prison Notebooks,* summarized in Smith, *Making the Modern,* 51.

66. Albert Kahn, "Architectural Trend," *Journal of the Maryland Academy of Sciences* 2, no. 2 (April 1931), 124–125.

67. Albert Kahn, "Architects of Defense," *Atlantic Monthly* (March 1942), 359–360.

68. George Nelson, "The Story of Industrial Architecture," in *Industrial Architecture of Albert Kahn, Inc.,* 7.

69. On this development in modern art, see Matthew Teitelbaum, ed., *Montage and Modern Life, 1919–1942* (Cambridge, Mass., 1992); also see Dawn Ades, *Photomontage* (London, 1986).

70. Benjamin Buchloh, "From Faktura to Factography," *October* 30 (1984), 82–119.

71. Ibid., 89.

72. On the relationship between twentieth-century architecture and Taylorism, see Mary McLeod, "'Architecture or Revolution': Taylorism, Technocracy, and Social Change," *Art Journal* (Summer 1983), 132–147. See also Charles S. Maier, "Between Taylorism and Technocracy: European Ideologies and the Vision of Industrial Productivity in the 1920s," *Journal of Contemporary History* 5, no. 2 (1970), 27–61.

73. Sigfried Giedion, *Space, Time and Architecture* (Cambridge, Mass., 1967), 254.

74. Albert Kahn, "Architecture: Whence and Whither," cited in Bucci, *Albert Kahn,* 178.

75. Albert Kahn, "Factory Building," cited in Bucci, *Albert Kahn,* 175.

1. Based on fragments of a report by C. H. van der Leeuw on his trip to America, c. 1925, quoted in *Leen van der Vlugt,* Weiderhall 14 (Amsterdam, 1993), 9.

2. "Van Nelle Tobacco Factory, Rotterdam, Holland," *Architectural Record* (1929), 387–390.

3. See H. A. J. Henket and W. de Jong, *Bouwtechnisch Onderzoek "Jongere Bouwkunst"* (Eindhoven, 1987), vol. 2, 35.

4. William Jordy has observed that the PSFS building is the most important tall building built between the time of the Chicago School and the postwar period; see William Jordy, "PSFS: Its Development and Its Significance in Modern Architecture," in *American Buildings and Their Architects* (New York, 1976), 52.

5. Quoted in ibid.

6. Le Corbusier, *Towards a New Architecture* (London, 1927), 50.

7. George Howe, in *Shelter* (Philadelphia, April 1932), 8–9.

8. In an article entitled "48 Systems of Prefabrication," entry A-27, under the heading "Frame and Panel Construction," was called the "Neutra Diatom." The illustration showed $1^1/_2$-inch-thick Diatom panels used for roof, wall, and base construction. See "48 Systems of Prefabrication," *American Architect and Architecture* (September 1936), 28–40.

9. Richard Neutra, "Systematics: An Ingredient of Design," *Architecture d'Aujourd'hui* 16, no. 6 (May–June 1946), 7.

10. Marcel Lods, "A Visit to Neutra," *Architecture d'Aujourd'hui* 16, no. 6 (May–June 1946), 5.

11. Richard Neutra, "Prefabrication and Personality," in *Nature Near* (Santa Barbara, 1989), 147ff.

12. Richard Neutra, *Life and Shape* (New York, 1962), 263.

13. For a careful account of this building's structural system and construction detailing, see Edward Ford, *The Details of Modern Architecture,* vol. 2 (Cambridge, Mass., 1996), 88–89.

14. Joseph Hudnut and jury, *Architectural Forum* (April 1935), 399; cited in Thomas Hines, *Richard Neutra and the Search for Modern Architecture* (Berkeley, 1982), 120.

15. Neutra, *Life and Shape,* 189.

16. Ibid., 223.

17. Richard Neutra, *Survival through Design* (New York, 1954), 57–60.

18. Ibid., 61.

19. Willy Boesiger, *Richard Neutra 1923–50: Buildings and Projects* (New York, 1964), 150.

20. Lods, "A Visit to Neutra," 5.

21. See Alfred Roth, *Die neue Architektur* (Erlenback-Zurich, 1946), 115–130, for full documentation of this building. Roth also illustrates one of Neutra's schools in the preceding chapter, 104–114.

22. Jean Prouvé, *Une architecture par l'industrie* (1971), 142.

23. Bruno Reichlin, "Maison du Peuple in Clichy," *Daidalos* 18 (December 1985), 88–99.

24. Ibid.

25. Jean Prouvé, "The Organization of Building Construction," in *Jean Prouvé: Prefabrication: Structures and Elements* (London, 1971), 24–25.

6 PREMADE—REMADE

1. Reyner Banham, *The New Brutalism: Ethic or Aesthetic* (London, 1966), 41.

2. See Hannes Meyer, "Building," in Ulrich Conrads, ed., *Programmes and Manifestoes on 20th-Century Architecture* (London, 1970), 117–120.

3. James Stirling, "Garches to Jaoul: Le Corbusier as Domestic Architect in 1927 and 1953," *Architectural Review* 118 (September 1955), 145–151.

4. Banham, *The New Brutalism,* 87.

5. Alison and Peter Smithson, "The 'As Found' and the 'Found,'" in David Robbins, ed., *The Independent Group: Postwar Britain and the Aesthetics of Plenty* (Cambridge, Mass., 1990), 200–202.

6. Colin Rowe and Fred Koetter, *Collage City* (Cambridge, Mass., 1978), 103, quoting Claude Lévi-Strauss, *The Savage Mind* (London, 1966), 22.

7. Lévi-Strauss, *The Savage Mind,* 21.

8. Alejandro de la Sota, *Alejandro de la Sota Arquitecto* (Madrid, 1989), 223.

9. Ibid., 74.

10. Peter Eisenman, "Real and English: The Destruction of the Box 1," *Oppositions* 4 (October 1974), 5–34.

11. Kenneth Frampton, "Stirling's Building," *Architectural Forum* 129 (November 1968), 45.

12. James Stirling, "Methods of Expression and Materials," in *Stirling: Writings on Architecture* (London, 1998), 129.

13. James Stirling, "Anti-structure," in ibid., 116.

14. Detlef Mertins, "Transparencies Yet to Come," *A + U* 325 (1997: 10), 4.

15. Sigfried Giedion, "Bauhaus und Bauhauswoche zu Weimar," *Werk* (Zurich, September 1923); cited in Mertins, "Transparencies Yet to Come," 6.

16. Quoted in *The Architecture of Frank Gehry* (Minneapolis and New York, 1986), 205.

7 TECHNIQUE AND APPEARANCE: THE TASK OF THE PRESENT

1. Reyner Banham, *Theory and Design in the First Machine Age* (London, 1960), 329–330. For a recent commentary on this passage, see Edward Ford, *The Details of Modern Architecture,* vol. 2 (Cambridge, Mass., 1996), 427.

2. Ludwig Mies van der Rohe, "Skyscrapers," originally published in *Frühlicht* 1, no. 4 (1922); reprinted in Fritz Neumeyer, *The Artless Word* (Cambridge, Mass., 1991), 240. More recently, and helpfully, see Detlef Mertins, "Mies's Skyscraper 'Project': Towards the Redemption of Technical Structure," in Detlef Mertins, ed., *The Presence of Mies* (New York, 1994), 49–67.

3. Kenneth Frampton, *Studies in Tectonic Culture* (Cambridge, Mass., 1996), 193–195.

4. Phyllis Lambert described the public approach to the building as follows: "This solution for the building has promise for terrific things . . . almost Baroque, you don't know what is there and then you come upon IT—with a magnificent plaza . . . a magnificent entrance to a magnificent building all in front of you." Quoted in David Spaeth, *Mies van der Rohe* (New York, 1985), 166.

5. Siegfried Kracauer, *The Mass Ornament* (Cambridge, Mass., 1985), 323–328.

6. José Luis Sert, "Windows and Walls: An Approach to Design," *Architectural Record* 131, no. 5 (May 1962), 132–133; reprinted as "On Windows and Walls," in *José Luis Sert: Architecture, City Planning, Urban Design,* ed. Knud Bastlund (New York, 1967).

7. José Rafael Moneo, "On Typology," *Oppositions* 13 (1978), 32–35.

8. Antoine-Chrysostome Quatremère de Quincy, "Type," quoted in Aldo Rossi, *The Architecture of the City* (Cambridge, Mass., 1982), 40.

9. The "case for figurative architecture" was made by Michael Graves in defense of a scenographic architecture that displayed historical motifs; "A Case for Figurative Architecture," in *Michael Graves: Buildings and Projects 1966–1981,* ed. K. V. Wheeler (New York, 1983), 11–14.

10. Aldo Rossi, *Scientific Autobiography* (Cambridge, Mass., 1981), 15.

11. Alan Colquhoun, "Typology and Design Method," in *Essays in Architectural Criticism* (Cambridge, Mass, 1981).

12. Rafael Moneo, "Postscript," in *Aldo Rossi Buildings and Projects* (New York, 1985), 310.

13. Ibid., 311.

14. Jacques Herzog, "Herzog & de Meuron 1981–2000," *El Croquis* 60 + 84 (2000), 22.

15. Moneo, "Postscript," 312.

16. Ibid., 314. Further: "Mimesis for him is not a mere repetition, but rather the effort to represent the common, the generic, that which implicitly carries an abstraction. . . . For Rossi, seeing things, representing them is knowing them."

17. Herzog, "Herzog & de Meuron 1981–2000," 86.

POSTSCRIPT

1. Immanuel Kant, *Critique of Pure Reason* (Riga, 1781), B 860–861; cited and translated in Caroline van Eck, *Organicism in Nineteenth-Century Architecture* (Amsterdam, 1994), 122.

2. Ibid., 123.

3. The basic texts include Martin Heidegger, "The Question Concerning Technology," in *The Question Concerning Technology and Other Essays* (New York, 1977), 3–35; Herbert Marcuse, "From Negative to Positive Thinking: Technological Rationality and the Logic of Domination," in *One Dimensional Man* (Boston, 1964), 144–169; Jürgen Habermas, *Toward a Rational Society* (Boston, 1971), chapters 4–6; and Arnold Gehlen, *Man in the Age of Technology* (New York, 1980).

4. Heidegger, "The Question Concerning Technology," 19–21; the same comparison is set forth in Martin Heidegger, "The Principle of Identity," in *Identity and Difference* (New York, 1969), and is interconnected with his arguments about both "sameness" and "belonging together."

5. Plato, *Protagoras* (Princeton, 1938), 320d–321d.

6. Le Corbusier, *Le Corbusier Talks with Students* (New York, 1961), 60.

7. Bernard Stiegler, *Technics and Time* (Stanford, 1998), 76–81.

INDEX

eden project.   cornwall